JOYCE DALE

CHILI RISTRAS *adorn the walls of many southwestern homes.*

THE
AMERICAN
SOUTHWEST
Land of Challenge and Promise

BRUCE DALE and JAKE PAGE

THE AMERICAN SOUTHWEST
Land of Challenge and Promise

Bruce Dale, *Photographer*
Jake Page, *Author*

PUBLISHED BY
THE NATIONAL GEOGRAPHIC SOCIETY

John M. Fahey, Jr., *President and
    Chief Executive Officer*
Gilbert M. Grosvenor, *Chairman of the Board*
Nina D. Hoffman, *Senior Vice President*

PREPARED BY THE BOOK DIVISION

William R. Gray, *Vice President and Director*
Charles Kogod, *Assistant Director*
Barbara A. Payne, *Editorial Director and
    Managing Editor*
David Griffin, *Design Director*

STAFF FOR THIS BOOK

Rebecca Lescaze, *Project Editor*
Rebecca Beall Barns, *Text Editor*
Thomas B. Powell III, *Illustrations Editor*
Suez B. Kehl, *Art Director*
Anne E. Withers, *Researcher*
Carl Mehler, *Director of Maps*
Joseph F. Ochlak, *Map Researcher*
Sven M. Dolling, Michelle H. Picard,
    Map Production
R. Gary Colbert, *Production Director*
Richard Wain, *Production Project Manager*
Lewis R. Bassford, *Production Manager*
Janet A. Dustin, *Illustrations Assistant*
Peggy J. Candore, Kevin G.
    Craig, Dale-Marie Herring,
    Staff Assistants

MANUFACTURING AND
QUALITY MANAGEMENT

George V. White, *Director*
John T. Dunn, *Associate Director*
Vincent P. Ryan, Gregory Storer, *Managers*

Elisabeth MacRae-Bobynskyj, *Indexer*

PAGES 2-3: South Window frames a pair of hikers and Turret
Arch in Arches National Park, Utah. For millions of years,
rain and frost have hollowed out massive blocks of Entrada
sandstone on this southwestern plateau. Erosion carves
windows out of the blocks, and windows further erode into
arches. Eventually the arches crumble to the ground.

CONTENTS

LAND OF LITTLE RAIN

WEATHERED WOOD, eroded rock, lichens, and a bit of hardy grass: Rugged elements of the American Southwest appear in Canyonlands National Park, Utah. The view looks south toward Elaterite Butte from a point waggishly called False Panorama.

ERODED BY WATER, scoured by wind, layers of red sandstone,

sculptured over time, metamorphose into a dreamworld of patterns and shapes.

SUNSET TURNS the autumn gold of aspens scarlet in Utah's Dixie National Forest, where

Mammoth Creek flows in the high country, as pure and inviting as the thin, crystalline air.

THE MOST BEAUTIFUL MUSIC in the arid American Southwest is the sound of water coursing downhill, curling and frothing sun-dappled over rocks, below stands of cottonwoods and willows. One of the most tantalizing sights in the region is a distant cloud trailing a streaked skirt of rain that evaporates before it reaches the earth—a phenomenon called virga. And one of the most terrifying sights is a wall of brown water raging through a slot canyon or into an asphalt intersection: flash flood.

Water. The miraculous substance that lightens as it solidifies; the artist-in-chief that carved the canyons, mesas, and buttes and shaped the mountains of the American Southwest. Long before it became a sculptor here, water covered the land and lapped at marshy subtropical shores plied by dinosaurs and their leather-winged kin. When this inland sea slowly disappeared, it left behind immense limestone reefs, fossilized bones, petrified trees and shells—museum exhibits of Earth.

Water. It was so precious that among the most common symbols of prehistoric human inhabitants were lightning, clouds, and frogs; so scarce that their descendants' chief artwork is still in the form of elaborate dances and songs that are prayers for rain. Water is, and has been throughout the time humans have lived here, the fundamental challenge—and promise—of the region we now call the American Southwest.

Here and there in the Southwest these days, you hear complaints about the influx of Californians, but this region owes its character in large part to California, notably the grand orogeny of the California Sierra millions of years ago that formed a north-south barrier and put the land immediately to its east in a rain shadow. Ocean-enhanced air, blowing in from the Pacific, confronts these mountain ranges by rising and giving up its moisture as rain, leaving dry westerly winds to blow across the land to the east. This creates desert, a place where the moisture that falls from the sky is greatly exceeded by the rate of evaporation.

In such a place, plants and animals have by necessity evolved methods of water conservation. Cactus pads jealously hoard moisture gathered by shallow, widespread root systems. A spadefoot toad can lie under the dry soil for two years until, however haphazardly, the rains come. When they do, the toad digs out, finds a puddle, and a new life cycle fast-forwards from reproduction to adult in a matter of days, leaving another generation of toads waiting....

If desert defines the Southwest, then Arizona is the region's center, for in that state four different kinds of desert exist. Leaking into the state's northwestern corner is the Great Basin Desert, which, interrupted with mountain ranges, stretches north into Oregon, a sea of sagebrush and saltbush with relatively few cactuses. With a base elevation of 4,000 feet above sea level, this desert gives way to a

AT TWILIGHT a pink and lavender spell lingers on the gypsum dunes of White Sands National Monument in New Mexico. A challenging site even for the adaptable yucca, the dunes continue their ancient march northeastward.

mixture of sagebrush and grassland that stretches across the Colorado Plateau well into New Mexico—or used to. Overgrazing has allowed sagebrush to gain hegemony in these semiarid lands at the expense of grass, so mankind has abetted the expansion of the Great Basin Desert into areas where it never was before.

Westward, mostly in California, lies the Mojave Desert, a land of scorching heat and low-intensity winter rains that are followed by a sudden flowering of annuals, some of which are too small to be seen with the naked eye. In the Mojave, widely spaced shrubs and the odd, branching yucca called the Joshua tree give way to ferociously dry moonscapes. One story has it that W. C. Fields, drying out in a Mojave Desert spa during the rainy season of late winter and early spring, came across a beautiful flower while on a walk. He called his agent, demanding he come, and the next morning took him in search of the flower. One of the millions of Mojave ephemerals that, like spadefoot toads, must live quickly, the flower was gone, the plant bare. Fields, it is said, beat the plant unmercifully with his walking stick, shouting, "Bloom, damn you, bloom!"

T WO DESERT TYPES reach up from the south and are named for two Mexican states just south of the border—Sonora and Chihuahua. The Chihuahuan Desert extends two arms northward into New Mexico, and lies across much of trans-Pecos Texas, occurring on land that, for the most part, ranges from 3,500

A TWISTED TREE needs only the smallest roothold to make a living in the red rocks of Arizona's Steya Neechee Canyon, once a place of swirling dunes of iron-rich sand subsequently compacted into solid rock and carved by erosion.

to 5,000 feet in elevation. In the lower elevations, creosote bush and tarbush dominate; at higher elevations, several kinds of dagger-leaved yuccas, and agaves, such as century plants, are found, along with grasses and a host of cactuses—mostly prickly pears and the heavily armed chollas (pronounced CHOI-yahs), which gained a reputation for leaping out to tear at the chaps of passing cowboys.

But the signature desert of the Southwest is the Sonoran, with its stately and clearly ancient sentinels, the saguaro cactuses, some reaching a height of 50 feet, their supplicant arms raised into the dry air. The Sonoran Desert begins near the Arizona border with New Mexico and spreads west across the southern part of the state into California. Typically at an elevation of 3,000 feet or lower, it is a subtropical place, receiving both summer and winter rains, however slight. Twice each year, the Sonoran Desert blooms with an array of wildflowers that seems miraculous. So diverse and relatively lush is its cover of bizarre plant forms that the Sonoran is often called "the green desert."

To begin with, the variety of cactuses is immense, ranging from the large, columnlike saguaro and the multistemmed organ-pipe cactus, to smaller, rounder ones with names such as teddy bear, barrel, and fishhook. Here, cholla cactuses become more elaborate than their Chihuahuan counterparts, and ocotillo, those peculiar collections of wayward, frondy stems, are all the denser, their red flowers of an eye-stabbing intensity. Shrubs have developed tiny leaves, the better to withstand drought, and the paloverde tree gets along for most of the year without any leaves at all, photosynthesis taking place in its blue-green twigs and branches.

Such trees serve as "nurse" plants, providing protection for immature saguaros, which will take some 15 years to reach a foot in height. A seven-footer is about 50 years old, and at 75 years it may sprout an arm. A multibranched 25-footer is a centenarian, and may weigh as much as eight tons. Generous to a fault, the saguaro provides nesting sites for woodpeckers (the interior walls of such cavities seal over with a woodlike tissue), and these will subsequently be used by purple martins, elf owls, and other temporary occupants. The fleshy red fruits, which grow following a period of nocturnal blooming, provide food and, if fermented, an intoxicating drink that has long been central to the annual rituals of local tribespeople.

In recent years, a considerable die-off of saguaro has caused some alarm, but it appears that most of it takes place at this subtropical species' northernmost range, where prolonged frost can occur. Young saguaros, particularly those shorn of nurse plants by grazing cattle, are susceptible to frost death, as are older ones whose structure has been weakened by generations of woodpecker holes. Adults, being so prominent and exposed, are often taken by lightning.

The western side of the Sonoran Desert in Arizona is one of the most forbidding places in the country; the single road crossing it is called the Devil's Highway, noted by an 1896 surveyor for its "painfully frequent crosses which mark the graves of those who perished of thirst." Only a handful of little-known water catchments called tinajas exist between Organ Pipe National Monument and Yuma on the California border. Even the late desert rat Ed Abbey would never go there in summer. Hapless aliens led astray into the region still perish there, and to the north the land is so desolate it has found use only as an enormous bombing range.

In season, especially in the eastern parts of the Sonoran, towering thunder-heads build up in an almost painfully blue sky, and lightning thrashes these desert lands with the regularity of a metronome. Sudden cloudbursts send more rain to earth than it can absorb, and it rampages downslope, gouging its pathway through loose soil, even rock. In season, too, the winds arise—relentless, savage—drilling tiny grains of silty sand into everything in their path, another of the grand sculptors of the Southwest. The hostile thorns of the cactuses, the spine-tipped leaves of yucca—these are only part of the violence inherent in the southwestern deserts, these parched and strange lands that go to such extremes.

Yet, in the frequent silence and stillness of the desert—any desert—it is easy to be lulled into a sense of timelessness, the notion that one stands in an ancient landscape that renders one's own life comparatively a mere spark. But the Sonoran Desert, as timeless-seeming as any, is only some 10,000 years old, coming into being only after the last thrust of the ice ages receded into Canada. Of course, far more ancient events prepared the way for the deserts of the Southwest.

*I*N EARLIER TIMES, the lands that make up the Southwest have heaved and buck-led, risen high, collapsed, torn themselves in two, and exploded with fury. Over eons, iron-rich red sand dunes from ancient seashores compacted into the great swirls now apparent in the thousand-foot-high walls of Canyon de Chelly in north-eastern Arizona. This is the same red rock formation that 70 or so miles to the north-west was slowly reduced to the templelike buttes and pinnacles of Monument Valley in Utah and Arizona, the quintessential southwestern landscape where John Wayne rode and from which Detroit has sold countless automobiles.

To the east, an enormous mountain once formed, magma later forcing its way up into its innards and along the creases in its body. In time, the mountain eroded away, leaving only a high neck of solidified magma and armlike dikes that stretch across the desert. This is Ship Rock, a reddish galleon that rises 1,500 feet in north-western New Mexico, a mystical singularity in the desert landscape.

A million years ago in what is now New Mexico, an enormous volcano erupted, dumping some 75 cubic miles of ash onto the land and forming the substrate of the Jemez Mountains. The mountains now ring what remains of the enormous caldera, a place called Valle Grande where cattle graze today. Not far off, in deep Frijoles Canyon in Bandelier National Monument, people carved cliff dwellings into the volcanic tuff some 800 years ago. The walls of the canyon, ranging from 400 to 1,200 feet high, are composed almost entirely of solidified volcanic ash.

MAMMOTH SLABS frame the buttes of Monument Valley,
which loom in the distance as part of an enormous sandstone formation
that extends 70 miles to the south to Canyon de Chelly.

THE GREAT Colorado River appears as a tiny trickle from this breathtaking

overlook a mile above the water at Dutton Point on the North Rim of the Grand Canyon.

In the high, semiarid lands of the Hopi in northeastern Arizona, flat-topped tablelands of yellow sandstone, called mesas, command the landscape like great ships in a frozen sea. Rock crumbling from their sides is strewn around them like immobile bow waves. On the horizon to the south, bizarre buttes rise from the tawny land, each one once a mesa now carved away by water and weathering. Each one will become—some day—a mere pinnacle and will finally reduce to rubble, almost as if rock, like water, seeks its own level.

About 75 miles southwest of the Hopi mesas, and always visible, rise the San Francisco Peaks, the highest point in Arizona and the remnant of a once vast volcano. In 1064-65, a nearby, smaller peak (now called Sunset Crater) erupted, covering the land with a layer of moisture-conserving ash. When people who were living nearby in pit houses returned, they found the land more productive, their corn and melons growing better than before.

Way to the south and east, in the Tularosa Basin, a volcanic eruption sent lava flowing across the land to coagulate into a motionless river of razor-sharp waves, domes, tubes, and fissures. The lava flow halted, shiny black, about 15 miles north of an alabaster-white dune field. Today the dunes of White Sands National Monument in New Mexico form part of the world's largest gypsum dune field.

The dunes were created through a series of geologic events that began 250 million years ago, when gypsum deposits formed a rock layer 500 feet thick at the bottom of an inland sea. After the sea receded, the rock layer uplifted as part of a massive dome. Ten million years ago, the dome's center began a collapse of thousands of feet, eventually forming a vast basin from which water cannot escape.

Water dissolves the gypsum from the rock and washes it down to the basin, where it pools into ephemeral lakes. Alkaline flats of gypsum and salts, called playas, are left when the lakes evaporate. As gypsum-saturated groundwater evaporates, a crystalline form of gypsum called selenite forms just below the surface of the playa. Wind erosion exposes the crystals, which crack and crumble in the desert's temperature extremes and blow northeastward on prevailing winds. Windblown gypsum is added to the eerie white dunes that move at a rate of up to 33 feet a year. Some dunes form in long ridges, and others in crescent shapes: barchan, with horns pointing downwind, and parabolic, with horns pointing windward.

Such relatively minor events have shaped the Southwest here and there. The landscape is a patchwork of such stories. The major shaping events have been almost unimaginably titanic.

More than a hundred million years ago, a large part of the earth's crust called the North American plate began to split off from Europe and head west where, in due course, it collided with the Pacific plate. The westering plate overrode the

FLOWING SERENELY below Toroweap Overlook, the Colorado River looks peaceable enough, but just downstream it will become a raging white torrent pouring over Lava Falls Rapids.

Pacific and drove it under, back into the earth's hot mantle from which it had come. The convergence of plates triggered an episode of mountain building called the Laramide orogeny, which resulted in the Rocky Mountains.

About 30 million years ago, during an era of regional uplift and crustal spreading, pieces of the earth's crust dropped down, bound on one or both sides by fault-block mountains. Eventually a rift valley formed, stretching nearly 500 miles from Colorado into Texas and beyond. Over eons the rift filled with rock and other sediments from the highlands on its flanks, and streams eventually coalesced into the Rio Grande, which forged a pathway to the Gulf of Mexico.

At about this same time, west of this vast tear in the land, a huge area of land rose as part of a regional uplift, creating a vast highland plateau that now covers most of northern Arizona and northwestern New Mexico and extends northward into Utah and Colorado. The Colorado Plateau, a circular platform of some 130,000 square miles, would soon enough become a textbook example of erosion, as weather and water attacked its softer rock, finally gouging out the Grand Canyon and thousands of other canyons, mesas, buttes, natural arches, and other geologic artwork for which the Southwest is famous. The southern edge of the plateau, rising 2,000 feet in some places, is called the Mogollon Rim (pronounced Muggy-OWN). Today what moisture arrives in Arizona in the summer, borne northward from Mexico, precipitates on the mountain highlands south of the Mogollon Rim and rarely passes above it onto the arid plateau.

In the vast jumble of mountains around the plateau, volcanism and igneous activity allowed mineral-rich solutions to rise from magma sources deep within the earth to fill cracks and fractures caused by the process of mountain building. This created seams and deposits of gold, silver, and copper. Hydrothermal alteration of copper minerals in the volcanic rock produced turquoise.

Between 15 and 8 million years ago, to the south of these volcanic mountains that now form Arizona's highland province and the great Gila Wilderness area in New Mexico, tension in the earth's crust caused it to stretch here and there and break apart. These tears brought about row after row of steep, mostly north-south mountain ranges like tiers of carnivorous molars, which began giving up rock and other sediment that filled the deep basins between. This is the Basin and Range Province of the Southwest, stretching from Texas into California—the site of most of the Southwest's desertlands.

Exactly where the American Southwest leaves off and the rest of the country begins is a matter, always, of debate. Some of the discussion smacks of xenophobic rivalry. Many New Mexicans are loathe to admit any of Texas, and some purists will go so far as to exclude that part of New Mexico—east of the Pecos River—

A MULE DEER fawn curls up for a nap in a high meadow in the Colorado Rockies. Within weeks it will lose its spots and will later follow its mother to lower ground in search of winter browse.

THE GRAY-GREEN LEAVES of brittlebush (opposite) show a reflective surface to the searing heat of the sun. In spring, this plant of rocky slopes is festooned with yellow blossoms. Its stems exude a resin prized by the Spanish missionaries as incense; Indians used it as a kind of chewing gum. The husk of a cholla cactus (below) ends its life in the desert looking like a piece of coral washed up on a beach.

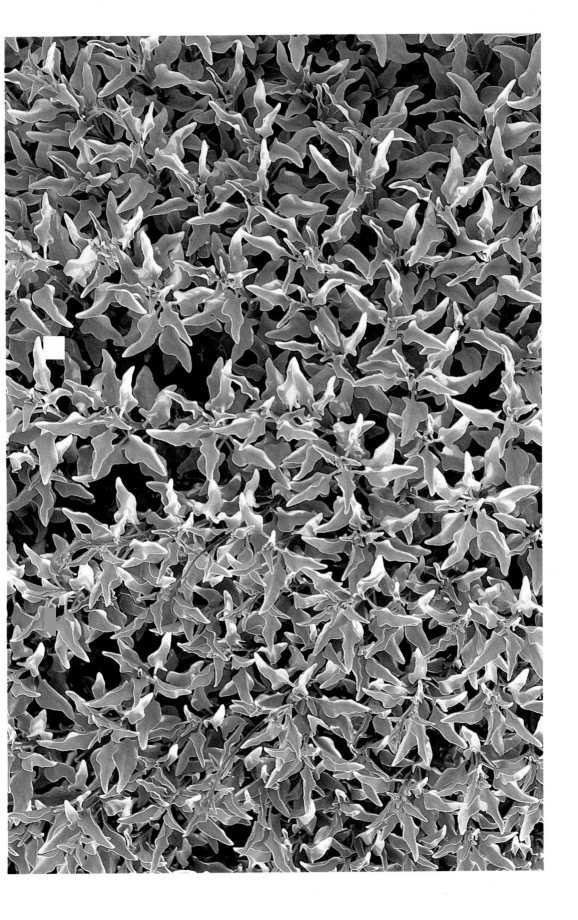

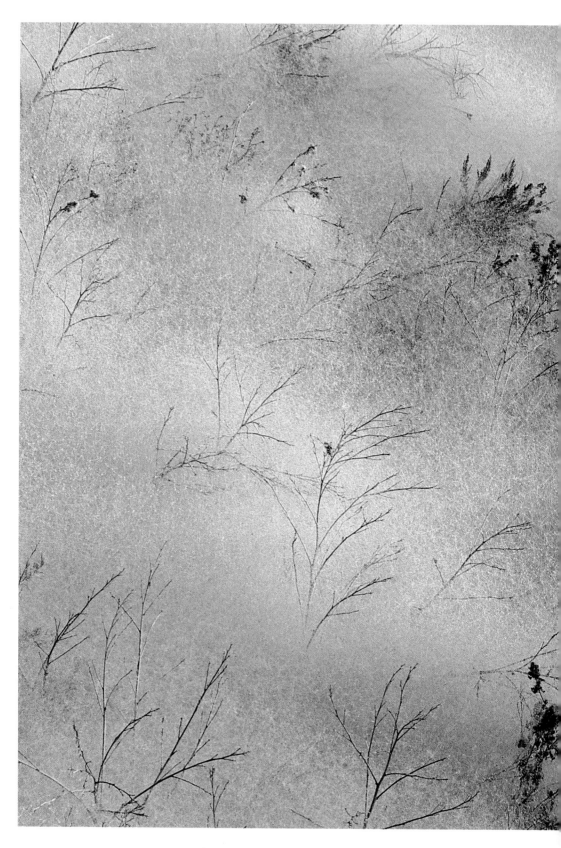

THE SUN SPARKLES on a pioneering congregation of airborne

seeds awaiting the wind that will carry them to a new frontier.

where the land has not been subject to much of the geological story told here so far, but is instead part of the Great Plains.

Some adduce scientific data—rainfall patterns, or the number of sunny days (much of the region experiences up to 300 and more days of sunshine each year). The Southwest, others will say with more poetry than science, is where the sky is never a milky blue but a blue of such clarity that it seems possible to see the emptiness of space beyond it. Others, even more vaguely, say simply that they know when they are not in it.

Yet, if one adds up meteorological, geological, and biological data—along with information about early human efforts at settling the land—one comes up, generally, with agreement. The American Southwest (which excludes similar terrain found across the border in Mexico) can basically be defined by the drainages of two great rivers—the Colorado River, beginning in the north where it is joined by the Green River, and the Rio Grande plus its major tributary, the Pecos. The one drainage system flows west and south to the Gulf of California. The other, draining southeastward, reaches the Gulf of Mexico. Between is the Continental Divide; By definition, it is the place that separates streams that flow west or east.

Within such a configuration, the political borders are not all completely arbitrary, as they are in the Four Corners area where, with a geometer's precision, four states meet at right angles. The border between southern New Mexico and Arizona, for example, is approximately where the Chihuahuan and Sonoran Deserts fade into each other. And it is along the United States-Mexico border where many life-forms that long preceded the arrival of humans found a natural limit.

SERIOUS AMERICAN BIRDERS can complete their life lists only if they visit one or two small pockets along the southwestern border in southern Arizona and Texas' Big Bend country, where certain Mexican species, such as the elegant trogon and the Colima warbler, appear in the United States. The same happens to be true of numerous reptiles, trees, and insects, including butterflies, but there are far fewer reptile, tree, and insect enthusiasts than there are birders.

Indeed, not far from the point where New Mexico, Arizona, and Mexico meet is one of the most diverse habitats on the continent—the Chiricahua Mountains. Here, long ago, a series of volcanic eruptions spewed ash that cooled and fused into a 2,000-foot-thick layer of rhyolite. The mountains were formed from the upheaval of this rock; over time erosion has sculptured the rhyolite on the western flanks into fields of pinnacles and oddly shaped columns called hoodoos. Among the artists of erosion that created this scene are lichens, which adhere in great tonnage to the rocks and trees. A single oak can play host to a dozen different species.

ONE OF 11 species of rattlesnakes in the Southwest,
the sidewinder ripples through soft sand, leaving parallel tracks at an
oblique angle to its traveling direction.

In the eastern realm of these mountains, winter runoff and occasional springs are enough to create a perennial stream, Cave Creek, which supports streamside species of trees and shrubs (and their inhabitants) that are quite different from anything a few tens of yards away. In this region of some ten square miles, one finds jaguarundis, six kinds of rattlers among 30 species of snakes, and 330 bird species, including one of the greatest diversities of breeding land birds in the nation.

Not only do two desert types meet in this area, but the northernmost range of certain Mexican species, and the southernmost range of certain U.S. species here overlap. Porcupines, for example, go no farther south, and coatimundis no farther north. Ascending the mountains, one passes as well through five distinct life zones that range from desert to what one finds near Hudson Bay thousands of miles to the north in Canada. For here, as in many other parts of the West, the mountains are sky islands, their upper slopes being today's relics of the ice ages.

*W*HEN THE NORTHERN ice sheets withdrew into Canada and beyond, the climate of the Southwest became approximately what it is today. Even in the relatively recent period ten to fifteen thousand years ago, when human beings first appeared here, it was a bit colder, wetter. Northern-type forests occurred, as did vast tracts of grassland, playing host to mammoths and other Pleistocene creatures. Later, bison roamed here. But as the ice withdrew, the cold followed it north. Deserts sprang up in the lowlands, isolating the mountain chains and the various squirrels and trees and other forms that had thrived here. New plants and animals invaded from the south or evolved in the heat on the drier land. Some of the earlier inhabitants simply moved into the mountains, developing over time peculiarities that scientists say render them subspecies.

One of the founders of the National Geographic Society observed this phenomenon in the 1890s, developing the theory of distinct life zones based on temperature. C. Hart Merriam, a Yale-trained biologist and later ethnologist, accompanied various federally sponsored scientific explorations of the West, including northern Arizona. There, particularly on the slopes of the San Francisco Peaks near Flagstaff, and in the layer-cake depths of the Grand Canyon to the north, he noted several different zones of vegetation. Based on average temperature, these also reflected elevation and, to a degree, precipitation. For it is the mountains and the cold air at their peaks that cause passing clouds to give up their moisture. Merriam's Life Zone concept has since been modified to account for the wide range of variables that can affect the distribution of species.

From sea level, such as in the depths of the Grand Canyon, to an elevation of about 4,500 feet, desert plants predominate. In the Lower Sonoran, desert scrub such as mesquite, creosote, and paloverde are dominant, but ocotillo and brittle-bush are also found. On the slopes of alluvial fans, where there is more moisture, succulent desert plants such as saguaro and barrel cactus grow, as do foothill paloverde and triangle bursage.

From 4,500 to 6,500 feet, in the Upper Sonoran, a pygmy forest reigns—mostly the relatively short piñon pine and Utah juniper, along with saltbush and grease-wood, all interspersed with grassland. Such areas have a spotted look not unlike a leopard's pelt, as British novelist D. H. Lawrence pointed out. Had he been a bit more attuned to the region, he would have said it was like a jaguar, which was once native and still makes an occasional foray here from Mexico. In the Upper Sonoran, where the average annual rainfall is only 10 to 20 inches, the familiar desert animals—jackrabbits, skunks, ringtails, lizards, and pronghorns (the American version of the antelope)—give way to mule deer and gray fox, rock squirrels and chipmunks. Cottonwoods, walnuts, and sycamores grow along streams.

The edges of these zones are, of course, inexact. Cactuses and yuccas may appear in the Upper Sonoran, as well as sagebrush. Which side of a slope one is on makes a difference as well—a north-facing slope being a bit cooler and wetter.

Above the pygmy forests of the Upper Sonoran, the Transition Zone rises to some 8,000 feet—a place mostly of pines and oaks, with silver and blue spruce found here and there. Gambel oaks and ponderosa pines tend to dominate, the latter with Douglas firs mixed in on the cooler northern slopes. Here, Abert's squirrels, porcupines, and mule deer are found, along with shrubs such as mountain mahogany, sage, and box elder, which go no higher.

Above 8,000 feet, precipitation may reach 30 inches a year, and the forest changes quite dramatically. Douglas firs grow densely, with quaking aspens and lodgepole pines rapidly invading areas opened up by fire. In autumn, the aspens turn, creating great swathes of gold among the charcoal green of the Douglas firs, and the ground is littered with their doubloonlike leaves.

At about 9,500 feet, where precipitation, mostly snow, can exceed 90 inches, Engelmann spruce and subalpine firs take over, with the occasional blue spruce and limber pine. In the upper reaches of this zone, called the Hudsonian for its resemblance to northeastern Canada, are the gnarled denizens of the tree line, including the bristlecone pine, longest living of North American trees. This zone is the realm of mountain lions and black bears; in season they descend in search of food, as do elk and, in a few areas, bighorn sheep.

Above 11,500 feet is a sixth zone, the Arctic or Alpine—a place of wind-deformed scrub, grasses, and a few very hardy flowering plants. Except for ambitious hikers, most animal life avoids this zone, which occurs only on a few mountaintops in the Southwest—notably the San Francisco Peaks in Arizona, Wheeler Peak near Taos, New Mexico, and part of the San Juan Mountains in southern Colorado.

When humans arrived in the Southwest—exactly when is a matter of continuing research and conjecture—it was already a place of startling diversity and stark beauty, of deep canyons, high peaks, plentiful game, wind-carved caves, and brightly flowing streams: a good place. It was also a place of violent changes in the weather, with killing cycles of drought, extreme heat and cold, and terrifying floods—a land mostly too arid to hold out great promise for the sedentary life of the farmer. But farming was, of course, not yet a gleam in the eye of the first humans who reached these lands, not yet part of the challenge and promise of the place.

A DUSTING OF SNOW turns the Pecos River monochromatic as it winds its way

along its 900-mile journey through New Mexico and Texas to the Rio Grande.

THE NEARLY FLUORESCENT red flowers of Indian paintbrush
glow among rain-dappled rocks near Colorado City, Arizona (opposite).
A distant thunderstorm draws a curtain of rain
across the desert landscape.

ONLY DAYS *after a brief autumn rain, the parched floor of the Sonoran Desert*

in Arizona transforms into a magical garden of wildflowers in bloom.

SEEN FROM *Big Bend Ranch State Park in Texas, the Rio Grande flows*

along its 1,250-mile course between the United States and Mexico.

THE FIRST ONES

FROM ANCIENT TIMES, people have etched designs into the face of Newspaper Rock in southern Utah. Human figures, animals, and symbols stand out against the rock's dark desert varnish.

By her fields on the Ramah Navajo Reservation in New Mexico, a Navajo woman displays two valued harvests. Corn adapted to high-altitude conditions grows well with the moisture from snowmelt and a few timely sprinkles of rain. A wild plant called cota yields a sweet beverage, a dye for wool, and a remedy for indigestion.

BENEATH A DARKENING SKY, wind-borne grains of sand create an eerie haze

around the red sandstone buttes of Monument Valley, a Navajo tribal park.

*I*N 1926, archaeologists working near Folsom, New Mexico, on the edge of the Great Plains unearthed fluted stone spear points and the bones of a species of bison now long extinct. The discovery of an apparent kill and the sophisticated weapons used to bring it down shed light on the earliest humans in the Southwest and how they might have lived.

Subsequent finds of larger and earlier spear points dating back some 11,500 years soon came to light in Clovis, New Mexico, and elsewhere on the Great Plains from Canada to Mexico, as far east as the Mississippi River. In addition to the finely worked flint points, early hunters made other points from the ivory of mammoths, various knifelike tools of stone, and rods of bone, which were beveled at both ends and crosshatched, for what purpose no one really knows.

These expert craftsmen seem to have appeared suddenly in North America. Archaeologists say it would have taken a long time to develop such tools, and they have not found any sure evidence of earlier regional craftsmen with such skills—though people had already dwelled for some time as far south as southern Chile.

By about 11,000 years ago, the Clovis points had disappeared—as had the large mammals of the Pleistocene. All across the continent, people adapted to new, dryer and warmer, conditions. Some had begun to move into the high, arid regions between the Rocky Mountains and the California chains—an area now called the Great Basin. These people relied more on gathering wild vegetable food than on hunting game. They collected and ground small seeds on flat milling stones called *metates* with handstones called *manos*. In addition, they used fire drills, small clubs, and throwing sticks called atlatls for hurling spears, presumably at large animals.

The people of the Desert Culture arrived in the Great Basin region some 11,000 years ago and were in the American Southwest—as far south as today's Cochise County in southern Arizona—by about 10,000 years ago. Theirs was clearly a far less dramatic life than that of the early hunters, noted for their no doubt electrifying, adrenaline-filled, and presumably collective hunts of huge game animals. But the desert peoples' ways of life were evidently more suited to the long haul: In some Indian communities today, women grind corn on metates using manos that are difficult to distinguish from those of the Desert Culture.

A few miles west of where the Pecos River meets the Texas-Mexico border, a side canyon cuts through limestone to the Rio Grande. Called Mile Canyon, it is on private property in the town of Langtry, Texas, where the legendary Judge Roy Bean, self-appointed "law west of the Pecos," dispensed turn-of-the-century justice from the porch of his saloon. Some 10,000 years before Bean, people ran bison through a natural chute and over the edge of Mile Canyon where the animals would crash against a rock outcrop, ready to be butchered and eaten. Bones of the period

THE TOWERS and kivas of Cliff Palace at Mesa Verde in Colorado were sites of bustling life from about A.D. 1150 to A.D. 1250. The ruins are preserved within what is now Mesa Verde National Park.

litter the outcrop to this day. Elsewhere in Mile Canyon, the floor of another cave is covered several feet deep with chunks of whitish limestone, the same rock type that litters the landscape above the canyon and gives it a disturbing, bleached look—mile after mile of rolling terrain, sparsely covered with hostile, spiky plants such as sotol and agave, along with mesquite and acacia.

Many of the rocks in the second cave were cracked in the intense heat of a fire. They had been used as disposable heat sinks in pit ovens, and they bespeak a major change that took place some 9,000 years ago in the lives of these former bison drovers. The ovens were adapted to changing conditions—a drier climate, fewer game animals, and, perhaps, a greater number of people trying to make a living in the same, now relatively marginal, place.

Once dug, a pit was lined with rocks, and a fire was built on top of them. More rocks were piled on top of the fire, and food was added to boil or was sealed over with dirt to roast. This is how these people cooked the hostile-looking plants of the desert, such as lechuguilla, a form of agave, with sharp-pointed, narrow leaves and a fat, shallow root. Lechuguilla yielded a poisonous sap for tipping arrows and could be torn into strips to make sandals. It was also the most commonly roasted food among the people of the time. Other foods among the many gathered were sotol, prickly pear cactus, and wild onion.

Archaeologists have learned firsthand that roasting lechuguilla for 48 hours in a rock-lined pit oven breaks down the plant's natural (and harmful to humans) steroids, rendering the fleshy parts of the roots and leaves edible. They have also learned that harvesting lechuguilla and chopping the tops of leaves at a 45-degree angle, hauling limestone rocks, and gathering woody shrubs for a fire involves hard work. As the climate deteriorated and game grew scarce, these early gatherers evidently had to shift to a more intensive means of using the landscape to survive.

A picture emerges—speculative of course—of small groups of people, perhaps a slightly extended family, sending out young boys to notify relatives of a feast. For days the adults have been out collecting lechuguilla, chopping the leaves, hauling the plants back to their cave in a canyon, along with limestone rocks and firewood. Relatives gather from far and wide, the oven is filled and sealed, and everyone sits around sociably, exchanging news about where deer have been spotted, where the acacias are putting out seed. Having this kind of information in such a changeable and inhospitable land would have been key to survival.

By about 1500 B.C., the first domesticated corn appeared in the Southwest—imported, perhaps traded, brought somehow from the tropical regions of Mexico. This new plant, which yielded small ears with tiny kernels, made practically no difference in lifestyle; life for the most part remained a seminomadic quest for food, fiber, stone materials, and seasonal water supplies.

By the beginning of the Christian era in Europe and the Near East, new tools and new strains of corn had begun to trickle into the American Southwest, mostly from the hotbed of creativity in Mexico. Pottery made its appearance in the Southwest around A.D. 200, providing a good way to keep food dry and safe from rodents.

Pots were less portable than baskets, but were more easily made and better suited for cooking. Storage pits, usually lined with rock, made it possible to keep food surpluses on hand for months, even years.

The population increased slowly, and groups that had consisted chiefly of nuclear families grew to include extended families. By A.D. 300, along the Gila and Salt Rivers in southern Arizona, people were living in small villages and digging extensive irrigation canals, a technique imported from Mexico. Squash and beans had been introduced along with cotton and gourds, and as harvests increased (perhaps from two corn plantings a year) and storage improved, a more sedentary life was possible. People began to accumulate material objects—expertly crafted pottery, traps, clothes, even jewelry. They bedecked themselves with beads, fetishes of various stones, rings and bracelets of imported seashells, and pendants in the shape of birds, frogs, and other symbols.

AT THE AGE of 111, Zonnie Henio of the Ramah Navajo Reservation still plants corn, shucks it, and cooks it in the traditional way. She also tends her flock of sheep each day and uses their wool to weave her own rugs.

One village called Snaketown was a year-round residence for 50 or so families in A.D. 300, a random complex of pit-house dwellings dug a few feet into the ground with poles holding up a roof of brush. Typically the houses had a single hearth, but some later ones had two, suggesting a multifamily dwelling. The town would grow and flourish for a millennium, but even as early as 300, the trend toward urbanization had begun in the Southwest—and has never really stopped.

Archaeologists call this irrigation-based culture Hohokam, and over the centuries it would spread from the south along the perennial rivers and streams of the region, reaching as far north as present-day Flagstaff by about 700. By this time, another feature (presumably Mexican) had been added—oval ball courts about the size of half a football field, sites of sport and ceremony.

Around 1100 things changed. For reasons that still remain obscure—perhaps an extended drought on the Colorado Plateau that led to diminishing river flow downstream in the Hohokam region—frontier areas were abandoned. Farmers moved away from the rivers, mostly into floodplains and up onto alluvial fans, and some multistory houses were built on the surface, surrounded by thick walls. Large platform mounds were built, often centrally located between towns, and burials reflected an increasing distinction between the rich (or otherwise revered) and the less so.

As Hohokam culture began to concentrate into a more limited number of locations, the previous flamboyance in jewelry and pottery design gave way to simpler forms. By 1450, the Hohokam culture was apparently no more, its villages abandoned.

A group of people living in pit houses and practicing simplified irrigation along the Gila and Salt Rivers witnessed the arrival of the Spaniards a century later. They were the Pima, a tribe that today refers to itself as the Akimel O'odham (the River People) and who are almost certainly the descendants of the Hohokam culture that flourished for more than a millennium.

To the east of the Hohokam settlement were the Mogollon, people who lived primarily in the areas extending from the Chiricahua Mountains north and east into the New Mexico highlands. Until about 1000, they lived in small bands in semisubterranean pit houses. Little clusters of these dwellings were usually built on high landforms, perhaps for defense, and large underground rooms were added, presumably for ceremonial and other purposes. While small-scale gardening was practiced, hunting and gathering wild food provided the bulk of the diet. The skills to make useful pottery were highly developed.

From 600 to 1000, the population seems to have slowly increased, and many of the villages were located on valley floors. The number of pit houses in each community ranged from a few to one hundred. Then, here and there, people began to build aboveground houses of stone, and by about 1300 pueblos were built in the region with as many as 500 rooms—many of them for storage—along with rectangular kivas and internal plazas. Individual families might inhabit three-room dwellings within the pueblo. Wild foods continued to be important, but the people grew beans and squash along with corn; such domesticated plants provided as much as three-quarters of the diet.

Migrants to the Mogollon lands included people from the deserts and from the plateau to the north, and tribespeople from Mexico as well, presumably fleeing the cycles of drought in those regions, and traders—all bringing new ideas and new designs. But some migrants could have simply been malcontents, or outcasts from other societies looking for a new start. Such things cannot be read from potsherds but can be imagined, given the continuity of human nature. In any event, Mogollon culture was something of a melting pot as long as it lasted, which was up to about 1400.

By that point, the pueblos had been gradually abandoned, some of them burned. The inhabitants are thought by some to have moved south in the 13th and 14th centuries to the Casas Grandes area of northern Mexico (also known as Paquimé). By the time people had given up and left the Mogollon region and Hohokam ways had disappeared from the archaeological record, the Anasazi had already left behind the most impressive architectural achievements in prehistoric America north of Mexico.

THE NAME "ANASAZI" calls forth images of Mesa Verde and Chaco Canyon, places where ingenious people built exquisitely crafted structures of stone, many within alcoves high up canyon walls. These were multistory dwellings, mysterious housing projects attuned with remarkable accuracy to the sun's daily passage. One can imagine early prayers in the dead cold of winter that the sun would, another year, decide to take up residence in its summer home.

The word "Anasazi" evokes romantic notions of an enigmatic past. In just a few centuries, this high civilization that was given to elaborate religious devotions came into full flower, then mysteriously disappeared, its stunning structures abandoned in the dry air and searing sun. "Anasazi" means "ancient enemy" in the language of the late-arriving Navajo. Today the Anasazi are also known as "ancestral Puebloans" or "ancient Pueblo people."

Until recently, it was thought that whoever inhabited these awesome ruins, these "stone cities," as people think of them, disappeared without a trace, and left no heirs. But in the past two decades or so, archaeologists have learned a great deal about who these people of the high Colorado Plateau were, how they lived, and what became of them. And if some of the Indiana Jonesian romance has been diminished by such patient troweling into their lives, the achievements of these ancient people remain awesome all the same.

They began, as did others in the Southwest in archaic times, with rudimentary tools for hunting game. They gathered wild seeds and fruit, following seasonal patterns and the generational variations of the climate they were dealt—in this case on the Colorado Plateau. They lived in pit houses, possibly in nuclear family groups, gradually taking on new ways—a bit of corn farming, the making of pottery—and no doubt finding guiding spirits and (Continued on page 60)

BEDECKED IN THE FINEST *beads, buckskin, and feathers,*
Indian children enjoy the pageantry of the Seventh Annual
All Children's Powwow (opposite), sponsored by Santa Fe's Wheelwright
Museum of the American Indian. A phantasmagoria of color and song
accompanied by the beat of drums, powwows held throughout
the nation serve as occasions to bring Indian people together, reaffirming
pride in their cultural identity. A wide-eyed baby takes in
sights and sounds at the Navajo Nation Fair
in Window Rock, Arizona (above).

FOLLOWING PAGES: *An observer at the Navajo Nation Fair displays*
his own finery, a bracelet on each wrist and a traditional Navajo
concha belt, all of hand-stamped silver with inset turquoise. The Mexicans
brought silversmithing to the Southwest; turquoise, a stone said to have protective
qualities, has been favored in the region since at least 300 B.C.

MARY CAIN, one of the
best known of the skilled potters
of Santa Clara Pueblo, holds
a redware pot with a water serpent
design incised and painted white,
a technique shown below.
She builds a pot from coils of
local clay and fires it in wood or
dung, as women in the Southwest
have for nearly 2,000 years.
Mary learned her art from her
grandmother and mother,
and has taught her sons, daughters,
and granddaughters in turn.

*A RARE male weaver among his tribe, Jaymes Henio of the Ramah Navajo
Reservation threads a piece of weft though the vertical warp of
an upright loom as a new piece begins to take shape (opposite). A strict
traditionalist, he uses only the wool from Navajo-churro sheep,
derived from the original breed brought to the Southwest by the Spanish.
He prepares the wool himself, carding and spinning it and dyeing it with locally
gathered plants. Rikki Francisco of the Akimel O'odham of southern Arizona
uses willow strips and a black fiber from a plant called devil's claw to
create a basket traditional in every way except for its size (below). Basketry is
the chief craft among the O'odham people, and miniatures woven of traditional
materials and of horsehair are highly valued by collectors.*

(*Continued from page 51*) profound meanings and mystery in the features of the land.

It was a harsh existence. We know from burials that a life of some 25 years wore a man down to the nubbin. Child-bearing women suffered more severely from nutritional deficiencies than their men, and children more than their mothers. People died often from parasitic diseases arising from poor sanitation.

Drought cycled in and out on an incomprehensible schedule. Wet periods turned seasonal streambeds into deep arroyos. The Anasazi learned to take advantage of floods by building dams to retain soil and nutrients for new fields. In dry periods, families moved to places where they knew moisture lasted longer under the sandy soil.

*T*HEY HAD TO HAVE BEEN a highly practical people, knowing limits as no lakeside or tropical people could. And living in their boom-and-bust world, gradually taking in more and more domesticated crops, they soon recognized the value of storage, of saving for a rainy day (or in fact the reverse), and it would not be unreasonable to imagine that they told stories to their children—moral fables—about ants and grasshoppers.

Not all Anasazi settlements were grand hotels of stone. At Black Mesa in northeastern Arizona, the basic unit was a rudimentary U-shaped dwelling consisting of a line of masonry-walled rooms for storage that were entered via ladders through the low roof. Two connecting wings with walls made of sticks and mud were entered from ground-level doorways. These spaces contained hearths and were living areas.

Just outside the arms of the U, or barely within them, was an underground kiva, entered from above, probably for ceremonial purposes, and beyond that a trash heap. There might also be a separate belowground room within the U for grinding seeds and corn on metates. Such a hamlet was typically located near a river bottom or wash where agricultural plots could be, at least seasonally, watered by simple irrigation.

At Black Mesa, a "mother village," perhaps home to an extended family, might have daughter villages on higher ground, places that had the same U-shaped configuration but no kiva. The people here no doubt returned to their mother village for ceremonial occasions, and archaeologists have speculated that these settlements were matrilineal, meaning in part that husbands came to live in their wives' places (still common today among Pueblo people). Beyond these outlying daughter villages, which were probably also year-round dwelling places given to dry farming and a good deal of hunting and gathering, were simple, upland sites where the people went in season to hunt or to gather piñon nuts and other wild plants.

If this, or something like it, was how many people called Anasazi lived across the Colorado Plateau from near what is today the glitz of Las Vegas to the upper Rio Grande, then from what sprang the sophistication embodied in these grand ruins? Chaco Canyon, for example, is close to the center of the drainage basins for the San Juan, the Rio Grande, and the Little Colorado Rivers, which lie athwart the Four Corners area. Here, from about A.D. 900 to 1150, a major religious, social, and economic network existed, stretching for miles across a most unpromising landscape. Centered in a long east-west running stream bottom in Chaco Canyon, this network included a large number of outlying settlements, many connected to the center by roadways so straight across the landscape that one suspects some sort of geometrical fanaticism may have been at work.

The center includes several major ruins. One of them, called Pueblo Bonito, is an array of once multistoried dwellings, storerooms, and kivas that opens roughly to the south. An architecture professor from the University of Southern California found, in the 1970s, that Pueblo Bonito was an improbably precise passive solar structure. Measuring the ruin's efficiency in admitting the heat of the sun into its various parts, he found that during the winter solstice, the efficiency curve is at its highest, and is flat throughout the day, allowing the sandstone walls to store the most heat for the cooler nights. And during the summer solstice, the efficiency curve is lower overall (as it should be) but is higher in the cooler hours of morning and lower in the afternoon, when the ambient temperature is higher.

Numerous theories and models exist to explain the rise and fall of the Chaco phenomenon. It is likely that it was no simple flow of events, but a complex history that gave rise to this complex civilization. Possibly its early major sites, begun in the tenth century A.D., including Pueblo Bonito, had primary roles as storage sites for food grown along the Chaco drainage. Stored food would probably have been shared in bad times with people from the surround. Also, at that time, turquoise was much in use, fashioned into beads and pendants: A great deal of lapidary work was going on, perhaps in some cases among full-time craftsmen.

Such jewelry almost certainly had a ceremonial role, but turquoise may also have been traded for food or other goods such as parrot feathers from far to the south. Chacoan-style masonry houses have been found near turquoise mines in Cerrillos,

PART OF EVERY NAVAJO FEAST, fry bread sizzles and rises in hot fat over burning piñon pine logs. The resulting aromas, mingling with that of mutton stew, are evocative of Navajo life.

south of present-day Santa Fe, and about a hundred miles east of Chaco, suggesting that Chacoans controlled the source and trade route of this valuable mineral.

Chaco, one imagines, could have come about as a religious-commercial center, with its ritual life devoted to engineering the climate (essentially prayers for rain) and finished turquoise being the chief durable item of symbolic, ritual, and economic importance. Thus, whoever the religious leaders were, they could command the cooperation of people to build ever more elaborate structures, staircases, and roads. The structures built between 1075 and 1115 included many added-on storage rooms, and agriculture boomed for another century. Except for a few short periods, most of this time was characterized by above-average moisture.

In this period, too, archaeologists estimate that only some 2,000 people lived year-round in Chaco Canyon, although residential rooms could have accommodated some 5,000 people. They also suggest that people needed for conducting ceremonies and perhaps administrators of roads, among others, lived there permanently. The other rooms may have been for periodic influxes of people on pilgrimages from the outlying communities, and for storage.

The system was clearly working: Roads were built to the outlying communities, which were themselves growing in number and size; the outliers brought food (domestic crops, wild crops, and deer) and other goods to Chaco, and the Chacoan residents performed increasingly formalized ceremonies that indeed brought rain. As long as the weather was fine, people would be delighted with the system.

From 1090 to 1100 and again from 1130 to 1180, periods of severe drought set in. The administrative center seems to have moved to northern sites—Aztec perhaps, nearer the San Juan River. By about 1150, Chaco was largely abandoned. There are no signs of violence, and the departure seems orderly, with useful goods removed. The reasons for abandonment are still unclear. A number of factors could have played a part, including drought, depletion of natural resources, warfare, factionalism, and changes in cultural and religious customs. Probably a combination of things was at work.

The ruins were set aside in 1907 as a national monument; today the area is designated as Chaco Culture National Historical Park. The Chaco phenomenon itself remains, in many ways, a mystery. Archaeologists argue whether the system grew elaborate as a necessary hedge against drought, or if elaboration occurred more or less naturally (as part of human nature) because there were periods of great abundance and thus the leisure to design ever more formal religious services and to calculate such things as the exact motion of the sun and stars. Similar questions are debated about the other great Anasazi centers—Mesa Verde to the north, for example, and Casas Grandes to the south. (Continued on page 71)

A SPIRITUAL LEADER of the Kaibab Paiute tribe of the Great Basin, Benn Pikyavit emerges from a sweat lodge. In this American Indian version of the sauna, water and red-hot rocks create a cleansing and invigorating steam.

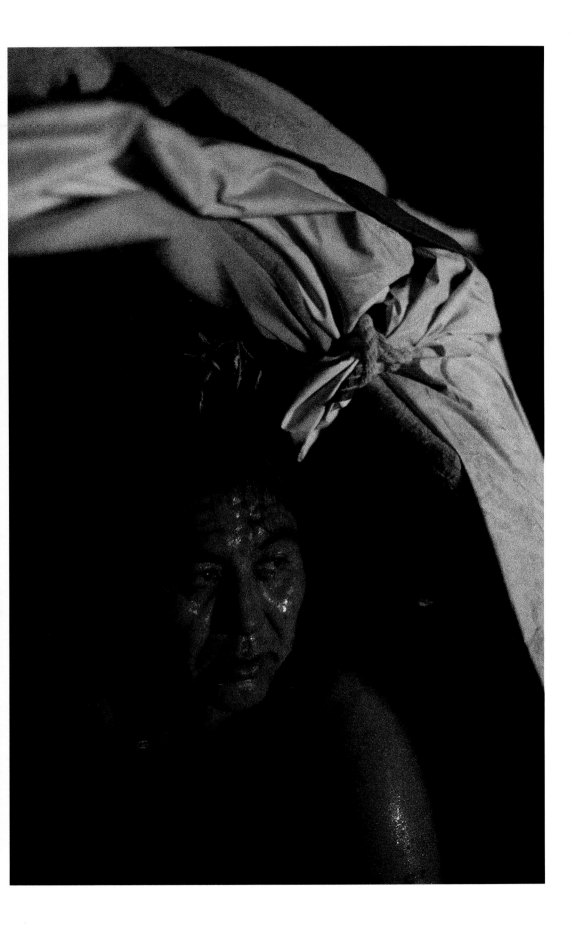

A JUMBLE OF BOULDERS still echoes history at Council Rocks in Arizona's Dragoon Mountains.

Near this spot, the great Apache, Cochise, made peace with the United States in 1872.

JOYCE DALE

ONLY RUINS *now remain of the once teeming, cosmopolitan pueblo of Pecos.*
Today a national historical park, it was once the easternmost of the New Mexico pueblos
and a major trading center, where tribes of the plains and pueblos met to exchange
goods such as turquoise, buffalo robes, and captives. The Spanish built a church
there as part of their missionizing efforts (above). Underground chambers called kivas,
entered from the roof by ladder, came into use about 1,200 years ago among the
Mogollon and Anasazi. Ceremonial sites for religious rituals and group activities, they
also symbolize a people's emergence from the world below. This one at Pecos
National Historical Park has been restored to its original appearance (opposite).

DRESSED IN BUCKSKIN and adorned with beads, porcupine quills, and pollen dust, 14-year-old Connie Rae Rice (opposite) awaits her part in the puberty ceremony on the Mescalero Reservation in New Mexico in 1991. The four-day ceremony, the most significant of Apache rites, ushers an Apache girl into womanhood. During the rite, the girl takes on the powers and qualities of White Painted Woman, a paramount and beloved Apache diety. The powers of womanhood are, in a sense, massaged into the girl by a medicine woman (below). Each day of the ceremony, the emerging woman runs to the sun at dawn and dances in the tepee until midnight. Accompanied by much dancing and feasting, the event is a time of both solemnity and great joy for everyone in the tribe.

(Continued from page 62)   It has been pointed out recently that Mesa Verde, Chaco Canyon, and Casas Grandes lie on almost precisely the same longitudinal meridian. Is it by coincidence?

And where did these Anasazi go as their world changed around them? After all, several thousand people don't just vanish into thin air.

THE HOPI INDIANS live today in a dozen villages on three fingerlike prongs at the southern end of Black Mesa, a vast highland in northeastern Arizona. In what we call their creation story—and they call their history—they emerged into this, their fourth world, from an underground third world. After spreading out across the land, they converged in what is called the Gathering of the Clans, all headed from the four directions and following ancient prophecies, toward their current home. The Hopi word for the people called Anasazi has always been *Hisatsinom*—ancestors.

During their migrations, the Hopi settled for relatively short periods of time, building villages, learning how to grow corn, beans, and squash, and taking part in ceremonies. In many of these villages, things eventually became too complicated. Priests, for example, turned humble prayers into overly elaborate ceremonies. In times of abundance, people grew lax and sinful. At such times—and there were many—some people determined that a return to humility was essential, and they would call for help from their deities. In some cases, the water serpent would visit sudden floods on the sinning village, and only the humble survived to move on.

North of Black Mesa in a canyon that is now part of Navajo National Monument, several cliff dwellings brood in the red sandstone. One of these, with 135 rooms, is called Betatakin, and archaeologists have determined, from tree-ring analysis of 298 wooden posts, that the nucleus of the village was formed in 1267. Three clusters of dwellings and storage chambers, corn mealing rooms, and fire pits were built then. A fourth cluster was built the next year. From such precise dating, and given such precise planning, archaeologists assume a previously united social group had moved in. Slow population growth probably continued to about 1285, when some 125 people lived there. By 1300, Betatakin was abandoned.

Today, Hopi clan members explain that Betatakin was one of the stopping-off places they inhabited on their migration, and that they left this salubrious place simply because their prophecies bade them to. Archaeologists agree. The Hopi—at least those who migrated to the Hopi mesas from the north—are indeed descendants of the Anasazi. As the great drought pressed the people harder, they moved to places where moisture was more reliable. Black Mesa tilts southward, groundwater trickling through and emerging here and there in small but constant springs.

IN A BLACK HOOD and towering headdress, a mountain spirit dances before a bonfire at an Apache puberty ceremony. At such rites, the mountain spirits perform the Dance of the Gahe to bring good fortune and drive away evil.

The long, shallow Rio Grande also beckoned. People from as far north as Mesa Verde, speaking a dialect today called Keresan, wound up in villages along the middle Rio Grande (in the approximate vicinity of Albuquerque) and to the west on a 365-foot-high neck of stone called Acoma—a fortress and eyrie to which water and any other necessity had to be borne up a precipitous trail. Among those early Keresan villages were today's Cochiti, Santo Domingo, and San Felipe. Some of these people may also have been from the Chacoan system, and some may have drifted north from whatever remained of the Mogollon culture. By 1300, similar villages existed along the Rio Grande from present-day Socorro all the way north to Taos.

Taos, Acoma, and the Hopi village called Oraibi are the three candidates for oldest continuously inhabited place in the United States. The Hopi say their prophecies told them to keep moving till they saw a star in daytime, which they did, stopping in their present area, and this suggests the supernova the Chinese recorded in 1054. This connection remains to be confirmed by archaeology.

All of these village people, regardless of origin, developed a similar way of life and world view. They devoted their efforts to agriculture and crafts such as weaving and pottery. Their ceremonial and religious life was a reflection—and engine— of this devotion.

There exist, from the 1300s on, depictions on kiva walls of spirit figures that came to be called kachinas. (In the Hopi language, Tewa, the proper transliteration is *katsina*.) The spirit figures, representing the forces and creatures of nature, danced in the village plazas and heard requests for timely rains. These dances are still held in Hopi and Zuni villages, and in great secrecy at some others. They are filled with color, chanting, the beating of drums, the clanking of bells and clacking of turtle shells. There are reverent observers and irreverent clowns, everything taking place under a turquoise vault of sky, in dusty plazas surrounded by ancient dwellings, the whole visible world a kind of cathedral. Such spectacle struck one observer, Vincent Scully, an art historian at Yale University, as the most profound work of art in North America.

*E*XCEPT FOR these pueblo villages, most of what is now New Mexico remained—for a brief interval—largely uninhabited. Elsewhere in the Southwest, people who called themselves O'odham, presumably descendants of the Hohokam culture, lived along the Salt and Gila Rivers, and some (the Tohono O'odham, which means "desert people") had spread out into the Sonoran desertlands south of those rivers, living in loosely formed villages, practicing agriculture at the base of *bajadas* and gathering wild foods in the deserts and uplands. These were called Two-Village people, and they moved seasonally from one to the other. Far to the west, where it was dry as bone, some related folk called Sand People simply slept on the ground, moving on in quest of the desert's sparse offerings.

From this region north, throughout much of western Arizona, in the mountains and canyons all the way to Grand Canyon, lived people who spoke a different tongue and had—some of them at least—almost surely inhabited these difficult lands for centuries. Highly mobile bands, they existed chiefly as hunters and gatherers, though they practiced some horticulture in season. Some of these people gave rise, it is assumed, to the Yuman-speaking tribes of today—the Hualapai, Yavapai, and the Havasupai, among others. These last have long lived in a deep tributary canyon to the Grand Canyon, a magical place of towering waterfalls that even today can be reached on land only by horse or shank's mare. Here, in the summers, they followed agricultural pursuits, and in the winter they climbed into the highlands to hunt game. There they often encountered and had to fend off their more warlike cousins, the Yavapai.

North of the Grand Canyon lived Paiute and other Great Basin people with simpler ways who soon took to raiding the settled and productive tribes to the south. Ute, as well, from the more mountainous areas in the north, descended from time to time to raid the settled people for their stores of produce and for their women—an ancient and universal kind of warfare. Such mobile groups as these, and the Yuman in the south, traveled light and left little behind for archaeologists to find and ponder. We know little about them from those days.

Nor do we know a great deal about the next great diaspora of people into the American Southwest or when, exactly, it took place. But it filled the vacant lands and soon changed the lives of most of those already here. These were the Athapascan, people who drifted down from west and central Canada along the great cordillera of the Rocky Mountains, arriving probably in the 1500s, though perhaps in a trickle a bit earlier. These people would come to be called the Apache, and some would later become Navajo.

Soon Apache lived east of the Rio Grande pueblos, stretching into the plains. Some hunted bison. Some lived to the north, hunting game and practicing a bit of agriculture in arid lands where Anasazi feet had so recently trod. Others spread into mountain regions, where Mogollon cultures had at least marginally thrived, and into the deserts of the south, pressuring by their very presence the O'odham and the Yuman. The Apache lived in small bands, following game and gathering wild plant food. They carried their goods in baskets and used dogs for pulling loads. They made weapons with great skill, from time to time raiding their neighbors.

In the south, those who would later be called the Chiricahua Apache disdained agriculture and anything else that called for digging in the earth. The Apache lived simply, without a chief; in times of great trouble a leader emerged and the bands would follow him voluntarily. They worshiped their own gods and consulted shamans for healing or for dealing with the supernatural world of witchcraft. They brought from their subarctic home notions that were quite dark.

The older tribes and bands in the Southwest learned to fear these rough newcomers, even though they sometimes came merely to trade, and even though they numbered just a few thousand in the entire region. Perhaps some of these Apache, in 1541, watched in hiding as men with shiny chests and headdresses arrived on fearsome animals no one had ever seen before.

Once again, the world was about to change underfoot as if in an earthquake.

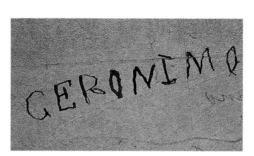

*GERONIMO'S GRANDSON Robert is one of many who trace their lineage
back to the legendary Chiricahua Apache warrior, who was among the last of
the free-roaming Indians to give in to the American government.
In 1886, Geronimo and all the other Chiricahua, even those living on
the reservation and those working as scouts for the U.S. Army, were rounded
up and sent east, where in Florida, Alabama, and Oklahoma
they existed as prisoners of war for 27 years. Geronimo (opposite),
whose signature appears on the back of a check at the Fort Sill Museum,
rode in Theodore Roosevelt's inaugural parade in 1905. He died,
still a prisoner of war, in February 1909.*

SUNLIGHT GLOWS *as if rising from the depths of the Chiricahua Mountains, long*

an Apache redoubt and still one of the nation's most biologically diverse regions.

THE SWORD
AND THE CROSS

WITH THE ARRIVAL of Spanish settlers in northern New Mexico in 1598, the cross became a ubiquitous symbol on the landscape. Tecolote Church was built near the Santa Fe Trail, the major commercial thoroughfare from Missouri that began opening the Southwest to American influence in 1821.

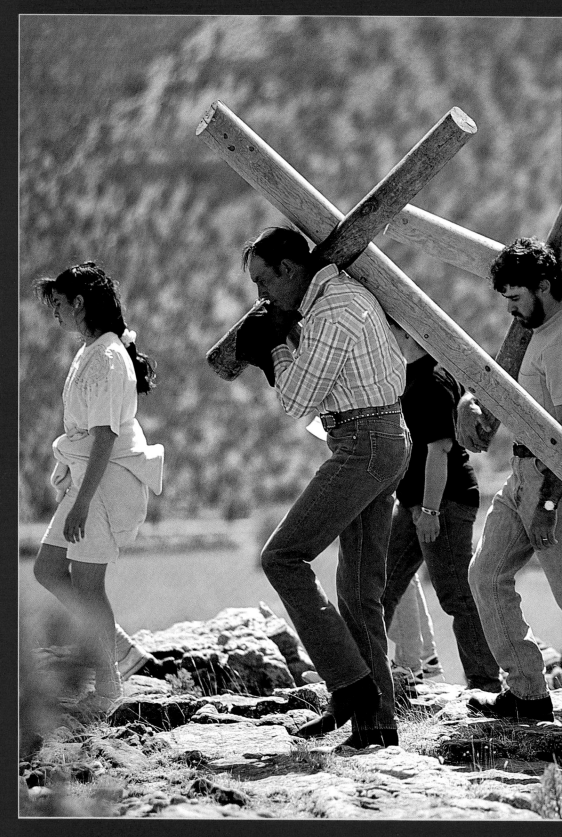

ON GOOD FRIDAY *men of Villanueva, New Mexico, carry pine*

crosses on a half-mile trek to a hilltop grotto that honors the Holy Family.

ADOBE OVENS called hornos, *similar to those made by Spaniards and Pueblo Indians, are*

still used in the Southwest. This one was stoked to make chicos, *dried kernels of steamed corn.*

THE FIRST NON-INDIAN to confront the inhabitants of the American Southwest may not have been what they came to call the "white man." He could easily have been a black man named Estéban who was a slave—but a slave with big ideas. In 1528 he survived a Spanish expedition from Cuba that had foundered in Florida. With three Spaniards he made his way on foot around the Gulf of Mexico, an eight-year trek that brought him to the colonial capital, Mexico City, which had until recently been the Aztec seat of empire, Tenochtitlán.

Along the way, among the various tribes these survivors encountered, Estéban became something of a self-styled shaman. Back in Mexico City, he and his companions told stories of great cities and great wealth, which fed the desire for that wondrous metal, gold, that burned so feverishly in the Spanish colonial soul.

In 1539 Estéban accompanied an expedition north into the high desertlands led by the Franciscan, Fray Marcos de Niza, to inspect these fabled cities and also further the other Spanish passion, the conversion of barbarians and savages to the Way of the Cross. Leaving most of the expeditionary force behind, Estéban proceeded with Mexican Indian auxiliaries into what were then Zuni lands, all the while sending tantalizing messages back to Fray Marcos. In this early boosterism of the American West, a Zuni village soon became "Cibola," and Cibola soon blossomed into a kingdom of seven cities, the fabled seven cities of gold.

But when Estéban reached this main Zuni settlement, a town called Hawikuh, he crossed a line of cornmeal at the town's entrance put there to welcome back Zuni from a sacred pilgrimage to outlying shrines. Evidently, Estéban did not realize the gravity of his mistake but went on brazenly to demand tribute—turquoise and women. The Zuni imprisoned Estéban and executed him three days later. Thus did early contact—by more of a con artist than a conquistador—end poorly, an unfortunate omen of things to come.

Learning of Estéban's murder, Fray Marcos retreated to the capital of New Spain, spreading word of a city to the north "larger than the city of Mexico." The following year, Francisco Vásquez de Coronado was dispatched to conquer these territories and find the fabled gold. He set off with a force of some 300 Spanish soldiers, 800 Indian auxiliaries, and hundreds of horses and other livestock. Four and a half months later, on July 7, 1540, the first group reached Hawikuh.

Among Coronado's first acts in this dusty, lackluster village was to demand food and clothing. When the Zuni refused, Coronado ordered the village sacked. Over the next two years, hardships accumulated, not the least of which were freezing winters. Disillusionment mounted over finding neither great cities nor great wealth, even on a long venture eastward out into the plains. The Spaniards repeatedly

WEARING HER FINEST for a birthday party, a young girl perches on the sill of an old customs house near Ribera, New Mexico. Here, officials once presided over the Santa Fe Trail where it crossed the Pecos River.

punished pueblo dwellers for refusing to give them food and other assistance, torching pueblos and burning hundreds of villagers at the stake. In all, 13 pueblos along the Rio Grande were destroyed.

In the spring of 1542, Coronado's expedition turned south for the last time, a resounding failure except cartographically. For a few decades, thoughts of northern gold fizzled like embers in the rain. But rumors of wealth never died out completely. A few smaller expeditions into this remote northern country took place in the latter part of the century. None had results that were satisfactory to either side; but they were sufficiently promising, it appears, that in 1595 the Crown authorized Don Juan de Oñate, the scion of a prominent New Spain mining family and accomplished soldier, to undertake the conquest of the north. By then, the King of Spain, Philip II, had ordered that the Indians be met with "peace, friendship, and good treatment" from the Spanish so that they could become willing Christian subjects of the Crown. Oñate was ordered, among other things, to take enough provisions so that no such burden would be placed upon the natives.

After considerable delays, Oñate ventured from Santa Bárbara, Mexico, on February 7, 1598, with 129 men, 7 friars, and 2 lay brothers, along with livestock and supplies hauled in heavy carts, fording the Rio Grande near today's El Paso on the last day in April. There, having crossed his Jordan, and amid devout prayers, he took possession of this Promised Land he would call Nueva Mexico in the name of King Philip of Spain.

At first, Oñate's *entrada* seemed propitious. During the expedition's parched foray across the sun-blasted Jornada del Muerto, a little dog, strayed from what may have been an Apache hunting party, approached the men, wagging its tail, and led them to a spring. Later, low on rations, they came upon two Piro-speaking pueblos that offered them large amounts of corn. Oñate in turn named the place along the river Socorro for the succor he had received. That same year, Oñate established his headquarters and capital in a Tewa village called Ohke (later San Juan), and established seven missionary districts ranging from the Hopi villages to Pecos, from Taos to El Paso—in all 87,000 largely unexplored square miles. A civilian leader called an *alcalde* was placed in each district.

In December of Oñate's first year in Nueva Mexico, the people of Acoma refused to deliver more than an insulting quantity of food to a passing Spanish expedition led by Oñate's nephew, a man named Zaldivar. In response, Zaldivar and 14 men climbed the 357-foot fortress of rock and began making their own collection, but the Acoma set upon them and slaughtered Zaldivar and most of his party.

Oñate reasoned that if such an act went unpunished, the Spanish would have no chance to establish rule over what they estimated to be more than 40,000 Indians in the province, so he dispatched Zaldivar's younger brother on a punitive raid. In the ensuing slaughter, some 600 Acoma were killed, the remainder hauled off to San Juan where they were all sentenced to penal servitude. In addition, men over the age of 25 had one foot cut off before going into bondage.

Military intimidation, then, was one prong of Oñate's policy; another was that Spanish settlers should live away from the pueblos, establishing their own farms and herds. Lastly, the Christianizing of the Indians was left to the Franciscan friars. With this tripartite separation of duties, the seeds of calamity were sown.

SOME 70 NEW SETTLERS arrived from Mexico in December 1600, having been promised a good life that included mineral wealth in the continuing boosterism from the north. But by the following year, 1601, a great despair had set in among the colonists. The land beyond the pueblos was poor, mineral wealth nonexistent, winters freezing, Indian tribute paltry, and the actual results of missionizing slim. Two-thirds of the colonists, risking charges of desertion, fled.

A debate that reached as far as Madrid followed. Maintaining this remote colony would, it seemed, always be an expensive drain on the royal treasury. But abandoning it might foreclose Spanish expansion northward for good and, as the friars and Oñate pointed out, if the Spanish left altogether, the Christian Indians would be murdered. In 1609, Oñate was replaced with a new governor sent to clean things up, and then was charged with inflicting barbarities and writing false reports. But for a few hundred Christianized Pueblo Indians, the history of this vast part of the continent would surely have been much different.

Soon settlers, friars, and soldiers began to return. The new governor moved the capital from Oñate's San Juan to Santa Fe, but the Spanish system inaugurated by Oñate continued and almost immediately threw all three groups into internecine competition—chiefly over Indian labor and tribute. The settlers themselves wanted nothing more than to become *hidalgos*, noble landowners free of taxation, with large herds of sheep and cattle for which the land was suited, and to be free from too much oversight by feudal lords. They were entitled to make use of Indian labor but were to pay for it. The Franciscans were free to use Indian labor to build missions and serve their other needs, as they were (it was hoped) converted to Christianity. Hardships encountered by the devout settlers and friars were to be taken as penance in behalf of the holy work of bringing souls to Christ. The governor and other officials expected to use Indian labor as needed and receive tribute from both Indians and the settlers. This group had no intention of staying permanently in so unfulfilling and remote a province, but merely sought to accumulate whatever wealth they could and return one day to Mexico, if not Spain.

In the certitude of their faith, the friars attended not only to conversion but to stamping out native religious practices—notably, the dances of the kachinas in smoky underground kivas the Spanish called *estufas* (stoves)—all of which was seen as immoral devil worship and witchcraft. Indian religious leaders were whipped (or worse), their religious paraphernalia destroyed. The governors complained of this treatment of the Indians, while the friars complained of the secular leaders' own misuse of the Indians and their blatant profiteering for personal gain.

The Indians soon learned to play these factions off against each other. Many times, to get even with the friars, the governors encouraged *(Continued on page 98)*

87

THOUGH PEACEFUL in the glow of sunset, the Pecos River, like other

rivers in the Southwest, remains ever the center of disputes over water rights.

A WELCOME SHOWER cools trail horse Mr. Woody and wilderness guide Huie Ley, a third-generation outfitter operating in New Mexico's 224,000-acre Pecos Wilderness. Ley, hat wrapped in plastic "to keep the felt from gettin' soaked," took over the business at age 15. He grew up in a town called Terrero, population ten.

CHILDREN HEAD HOME from the bus stop in Sena, New Mexico, passing the town's only store. Along the road, an irrigation ditch called an acequia *serves the town's agricultural needs, conveying water from the nearby Pecos River. Many of the acequias in use today date back to the time of the original settlers, and in a number of river towns, a* mayordomo, *or ditch boss, still oversees their use.*

"FANDANGOS, *as they are
sometimes called, are carried
on almost every night.
The love of the people for
dancing is almost insatiable...."
So wrote visitor William A. Bell
in* 1869. *His observation still
holds true, as this dance
during a festival in Las Vegas,
New Mexico, shows.*

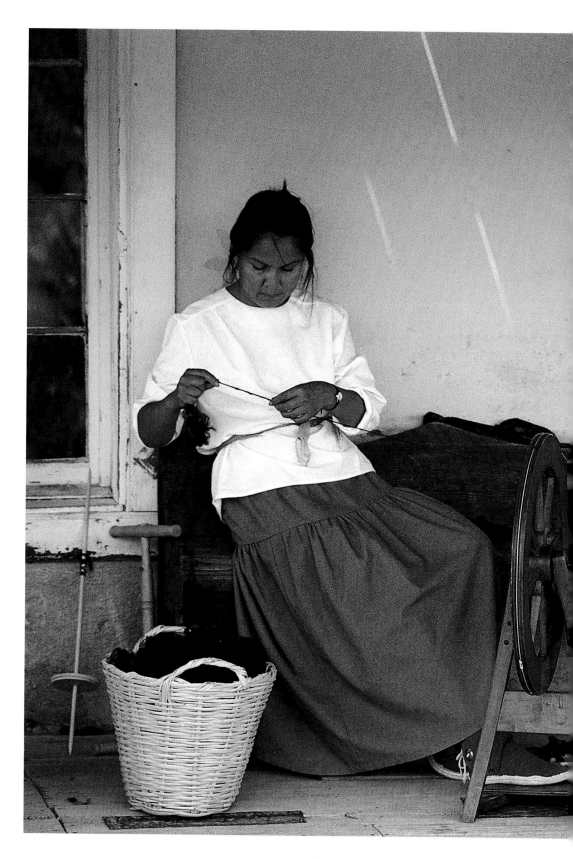

IN PERIOD COSTUME, *a
woman demonstrates spinning
techniques (left) at El Rancho
de Las Golondrinas, a restored 18th-
century village and working
ranch near Santa Fe, New Mexico.
Shearing sheep (below)
for wool has been part of life in
the Southwest since the first
Spanish colonists brought flocks to
New Mexico in 1598.*

(Continued from page 87) the Indians to flout the holy men by practicing their pagan rites. For some 70 years, accusations flew back and forth, and the various Pueblo tribes alternately acceded to Spanish strictures, openly resisted, or simply went underground, while governors came and went, reluctantly serving in this desolate and discouraging outpost.

The tinderbox situation was by no means calmed by nomadic tribes, who were much more efficient after the rapid adoption of the Spanish horse and who profited from the addition of livestock to the region. Both Spanish and Indian herds were compelling targets, as were the triennial pack trains that brought supplies from distant Mexico and returned with trade goods.

By 1680, the situation in Nueva Mexico had reached its lowest ebb. A severe drought in the late 1660s and early 1670s that left the people eating the leather tack of their horses, along with increasingly bold raids by outlying tribes, had brought about a period of grudging cooperation between Spanish factions. The military even assisted friars in 1675 in publicly whipping 43 Pueblo religious leaders and hanging 3 others for encouraging idolatry. Indian anger seethed, finally reaching such a boiling point that the pueblos—from Taos west to the remote Hopi mesas—rose up in rebellion.

One of the humiliated Indian priests was a man named Popé from San Juan Pueblo, formerly called Ohke. He went underground, hiding in Taos. With the help of other determined leaders, possibly including a charismatic black slave named Naranjo who had gone to live among the Indians, he plotted the rebellion for years. Finally in the summer of 1680, it was time. Messengers ran across the land among the pueblos carrying knotted ropes, each knot representing a day until the revolt. Pueblos were warned to join or to be destroyed by the rebels. Most joined. At the time, some 2,500 Spanish settlers and troops and some 30 friars lived among six times that many Pueblo people along the Rio Grande drainage, plus those at Acoma, Zuni, and Hopi to the west.

The Spanish governor, Antonio de Otermín, received word of the imminent uprising, but Popé advanced the time of the rebellion. Early on the morning of August 10, 1680, the Pueblo struck with a unity of purpose that was unprecedented in their long history.

In the little pueblo of Tesuque, a few miles north of Santa Fe, a friar called Father Pio rode toward the village in the company of a single soldier in a cameo reminiscent of Cervantes' Don Quixote and Sancho Panza. Some of the friar's Tesuque flock appeared, their faces painted. The soldier watched as Father Pio followed them around a bend, calling to them. Moments later, the Indians reappeared, covered with blood, and the soldier fled back to Santa Fe to alert the governor.

In the next two days, up and down the Rio Grande and out to the west, the Pueblo people killed the friars in their midst, burned the missions, and went on to sack nearby *haciendas*, driving the surviving northern settlers to the walled safety of Santa Fe. While settlers south of present-day Albuquerque fled farther south, Indians soon surrounded Santa Fe. A siege of the capital ensued, with Otermín and the surviving Spanish finally breaking out to begin the long and degrading march out of the once promised land of Nueva Mexico to languish near El Paso. They were joined by some Christianized Indians, particularly from the pueblo of Isleta, and were watched along their lugubrious journey by the rebels. They were not greatly harassed, except by Apache in the south. The purpose of the Pueblo Rebellion of 1680 was not to slaughter the hated oppressors so much as to see them leave the territory.

*I*N THIS GOAL, the Indians failed, for the Spanish returned in force 12 years later. Nor did Pueblo unity survive. Popé and other leaders soon showed signs of tyranny and were discredited. Such attitudes as overweening pride have never been taken as virtues among the Indian people. The Spanish returned under a new governor, Diego de Vargas, to find a world in disarray, numerous pueblos abandoned, and others removed to higher, safer ground. Old hostilities that always simmered among the fractious Pueblo tribes had flamed again. Many people had fled, some to Hopi lands, where they hoped to establish a new life. Apache raids had resumed. Many of the tribes were quick to welcome the Spaniards back; others resisted and were routed, often with the aid of neighboring Pueblo tribes now loyal again to Spain.

Relative calm returned over the next few years. New missions arose in the pueblos, most of which also accepted a Spanish form of governance that split religious and secular duties between different local leaders, thus adding to but not replacing the firm theocracy of tradition. But it became clear that the Pueblo Rebellion had succeeded in one important way. No longer did the Franciscan friars see it as a practical part of their mission to stamp out the kachinas and the rest of Pueblo religion.

Indians were no longer punished for not attending Mass; kachinas danced in the plazas without harassment. There began an informal system of cooperation, or at least benign neglect, and the two religions entered a period of coexistence that continues today. The Pueblo father-creator, after all, was not so different from the Catholic God, the Pueblo goddesses of the land not unlike the Virgin so central to Spanish *catholicismo*, and the kachinas—were they so different from angels and saints? Pueblos celebrated the feast days of their patron saints with an early morning Mass and then carried the saint's statue ceremoniously from church to plaza where the people danced throughout the day. Indeed, in the century following the Pueblo Rebellion, the missionary fervor of the Franciscans dwindled to a vanishing point, and mutual tolerance became the order of the day—and still is.

The pueblo population had dropped by almost half, and would halve again in the next century. Many fled the area; others died in continuing outbreaks of European-borne disease. But it is to the Pueblo Rebellion of 1680 and its chastening effect on Spanish missionary fervor that the Rio Grande pueblo people, with considerable pride, attribute the remarkable continuity of their traditional cultures.

Yet another major result of the Pueblo Rebellion was the emergence of some Apachean bands to the northwest of the Rio Grande pueblos as a distinct culture:

the Navajo. Today the Navajo are by far the largest tribe in the Southwest in land and population; in the late 16th century they were a few loosely associated bands of people located uneasily in the San Juan River basin between the Ute and the Rio Grande pueblos, dependent mostly on hunting and gathering wild food.

When the Spanish returned in 1692, they met with some resistance, nowhere more determined than among the Jemez people, whose pueblos were located in the mountainous area west of the Rio Grande. In the ensuing warfare, many from Jemez fled to live among the Navajo. Some returned later, but many stayed on and inter-married. Soon Navajo were weaving, making pueblo-style pottery, building small stone villages (*pueblitos*) as defense against the ever more threatening Ute, and adding kachina dances, sandpaintings, and other features of more organized pueblo life and religion to their largely shamanistic ways. They retained their Apachean tongue and their own ceremonial six- or eight-sided structures called hogans (pro-nounced HOE-gahns).

Also mixed in were European elements—sheep, cattle, goats, the use of metal, and cotton. Later in the 18th century, the Navajo would shed some pueblo elements—the multicolored pottery, pueblitos, kachinas—but they were now a new people, pastoralists, with a proven ability to adapt rapidly and take on whatever they desired from surrounding people, ignoring the rest. The Spanish never succeeded in mis-sionizing them, for example, or imposing any kind of political control.

WHEN COLONIAL EXPANSION brought Spanish haciendas and ranches into the lands of the Navajo, there were raids and counter-raids for live-stock, slaves, and revenge. The Navajo grew in number, powerful and troublesome thorns in the side of the colonists and their pueblo allies.

It was the Apache, however, in the southern and western portions of Nueva Mexico, and the Yuman-speaking Yavapai (with whom Apache were often con-fused) that kept the Spanish out of most of what is now Arizona. Spanish pene-tration there was restricted largely to what was called the Pimería Alta, the desertlands of the Papago and the Pima in northern Sonora and southern Arizona to today's Tucson. It was accomplished much later, and in a manner unlike the Spanish thrust into the lands of the Rio Grande.

Jesuits, not Franciscans, had missionized the Mexican Indian tribes that lay south of today's Arizona, and the Jesuit approach was different in several impor-tant particulars. They tended to arrive amidst a new group of Indians, bringing cattle, sheep, goats, or other livestock with them as tangible benefits, as well as the seeds for new crops such as wheat. Immediately, they began to preach, telling attractive stories from the Bible and demonstrating fascinating new rituals. The purpose, beyond saving souls, was to cause villages to form around a mission, and to convert the free-ranging tribal people to a more orderly and settled way of life in service to the missionary, the Church, and the Crown—in short, to make them citizens of towns and thus of a distant nation.

Into the most northern realms of those Indians the Spanish called Pima came an ebullient and energetic salesman, an Italian Jesuit in his forties named Eusebio Francisco Kino. He began his missionary work in 1687 while the one-time New Mexicans languished in El Paso, dreaming of their return. Wise to the conflicting interests of settlers and missionaries over the use of Indian labor, Father Kino arrived bearing an order from the viceroy of New Spain that disallowed forced Indian labor and exempted Indians from tribute while the missionary program was under way.

Instead of establishing a mission and staying on there, Father Kino traveled extensively among the northern Piman people, from the San Pedro River all the way west to the Colorado River. He was both persuasive and patient. Unlike many other missionaries, he was content to sit for days and nights, listening to Indian elders talk, then taking his turn. Generally, he was accorded an enthusiastic welcome. The Indians, hearing he was coming, often erected crosses to honor him, and he would send word back to New Spain that another group would welcome a missionary to come and establish a church in their midst. Then he would move on to another place. He was as much an explorer as a missionary, determining for instance that California was not an island, as was then believed.

The establishment of new missions and missionaries in the Pimería Alta region never did catch up with Kino's sales pitch. For example, in the 1690s, Kino established both a large cattle herd among the Indians near Bac (south of Tucson) and a great desire for a missionary. He did begin a rudimentary mission church, named for his patron saint, San Xavier, a missionary who died in Asia and whose body, shipped home to Europe, miraculously arrived without having decomposed. At Kino's death in 1711, the Indians around Bac still had an incomplete mission and no regularly visiting missionary—and still didn't as late as 1730. By then, some 20 missions and *visitas* (places for visiting missionaries) had dropped to nine.

Settlers from the south soon arrived in the region west of the Santa Cruz River, and conflict between them and the flagging missionary effort soon erupted, along with violent uprisings on the part of disgruntled Piman groups, a major one taking place in 1751. There was also increasingly frequent raiding by Apache directly to the east—raids on both Indian and Spanish neighbors that led to a general atmosphere of terror along this northern frontier of Spanish imperial expansion.

In 1767, in a grand reorganization of the Church's missionary efforts, the Jesuit order was banished from the New World, and Franciscans took on the few remaining missions among the Piman people, chiefly at San Xavier del Bac and a bit south at Tumacacori. At the former, the Franciscans began in 1783 to erect a new church, now known as "The White Dove of the Desert," an elaborate twin-towered blend of baroque, Moorish, and Byzantine design filled with paintings on the walls and ceiling, *retablos* (painted wooden panels), and statuary in a reverent riot of bright reds, deep blues, yellows, silver, and gold. Two centuries after its completion in 1797, a local group mounted a two-million-dollar international restoration of the church, considered by some to be "the Sistine Chapel of the United States." The church stands within the San Xavier Indian Reservation, where it continues to serve the spiritual needs of its Papago (now Tohono O'odham) parishioners.

As other family members relax along the Rio Grande on the

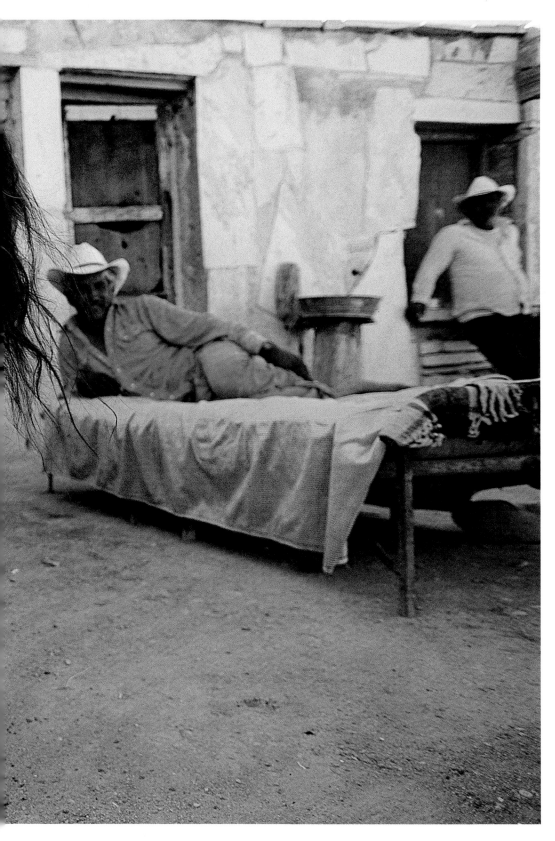

Mexican border, a mother dips her reluctant infant into a makeshift bathtub.

Before the White Dove was begun and only four months or so after Paul Revere's ride out of Boston in 1775, an Irishman called Don Hugo O'Connor designated a spot along the Santa Cruz River ten miles north of Bac as the site for a new presidio, a military outpost that would help defend the territory against raiding Apache. It was at the foot of a large hill of black volcanic rock for which a local word was *stjukson*, and it became known as Tucson. A thickly walled fort, it soon became the center for a few Spanish and Piman settlers who farmed along the river. While the Spanish mounted a few expeditions farther north, one of them reaching as far as the lands of the Paiute, this Presidio of San Augustín del Tucson was as far north into Arizona as Spanish settlement would reach.

Today the Rio Grande is a tame river, its course punctuated by several dams that regulate its flow, but as domesticated as it is, it still creates a green swath down the entire length of New Mexico. For millennia this ribbon of green has been seen from above by a multitude of sandhill cranes and snow geese, flying in to winter in wetlands along the river's edge, gathering up in a great spectacle in spring to return to breeding grounds in the north. For the birds, the river created a lush and welcoming place amid the dry and hostile lands beyond it. And so, to a degree, did the river provide a forgiving strip for the remaining Pueblo people and the Hispano colonists (those descended from early Spanish settlers). In the years following the Pueblo Rebellion, the Hispanos filled in the lands between pueblos and took over those regions abandoned by the Pueblo people south of the provincial capital, Santa Fe.

Up and down the Rio Grande, the settlers lined the river's edge with irrigation ditches called *acequias*, like veins draining water from an *acequia madre* into the fields. These, plus the annual deposits of rich silt from the river's spring floods, particularly in the Rio Baja, south of Santa Fe down to today's Las Cruces, made farming the likes of chili, wheat, corn, and other crops possible. Towns such as Tome and Belen grew, surrounded by green fields, with large herds of cattle and sheep ranging in nearby grasslands that stretched into the foothills of mountain chains at the edge of the Rio Grande Rift Valley. Each such town elected a *mayordomo*, or ditch boss, who oversaw the annual cleaning out of the irrigation ditches and saw to it that no one kept ditch gates open longer than was proper. The mayordomo was, in fact, a separate and independent official, in effect another layer of government. Many of the Pueblo adopted this office from the settlers, and the ditches in a number of river towns today still are ruled by mayordomos.

Some of the hidalgos, and particularly those in the south, grew relatively wealthy—at least compared to others in the region who were less fortunate. These few could afford clothes manufactured in Chihuahua to the south—nothing like the

LACE, FLOWERS, AND FINERY are all part of a quinceañera, *a traditional party that celebrates a girl's 15th birthday with music, dancing, and feasting.*

finery with which the original conquistadors had bedecked themselves, but still far more elegant than the skins and rough cloth that most New Mexicans wore. Here life would go on for almost two centuries without much change—a simple, provincial, tradition-bound agricultural and pastoral round threatened always by wayward shifts in the climate and, of course, the attentions of raiding parties.

In the north, however, with the exception of Santa Fe itself, life was even harder, not merely because of a shorter growing season in the higher elevations. By the middle of the 18th century, the Apache bands in the northeast (those that would come to be called the Jicarilla Apache) had begun to take on some sedentary ways from their Pueblo and Hispano neighbors—in particular from the cosmopolitan trading pueblo of Pecos—and posed a diminishing threat. But this vacuum was soon filled by Comanche, sometime allies of the Ute who had recently streamed out of the Great Basin into the nearby plains and took after their new neighbors, first Apache, then Pueblo and Hispano alike—raiding, slaving, working their will with an unrivaled ferocity. In this, they were greatly aided by the possession of firearms far more modern than any owned by the settlers, which the raiders received in happy trade with the French who were nosing southward into the plains.

The governors of New Mexico and its ill-armed military were largely helpless against this new force, and aid from New Spain would be stingy: The grand dreams for New Mexico were long over. From the standpoint of both secular and religious imperialism, it was what today would be called a rathole. Its only real value to Spain was that it was not owned by any other power but constituted a spindly barrier against the expected arrival of French, Russians, or English into the region.

It is unlikely that any but a few New Mexicans were aware of the grand movements and machinations of empires, so isolated were they from the rest of the world and so preoccupied with their own survival. Many still spoke Spanish that sounded much like 16th-century Castilian, just as hollow-dwelling Kentuckians spoke something like Elizabethan English until this century. Most New Mexicans still hauled goods in wooden-wheeled carts, so rare were iron and blacksmithing.

From such anachronistic elements, however, a new society was nevertheless arising. It was based largely on genealogy, and at the top were those who claimed direct and pure descent from the Spaniards who had arrived with Coronado and other early colonial expeditions. This aristocratic element tended to be centered in Santa Fe (which still retains a sense of being somehow above the rest of the state), and many of the hidalgos to the south could claim such ancestry. A distinction was made between those *españoles* who were born in Spain (*peninsulares*) or in Mexico (*criollos*). Not until the late 20th century did some of these old Spanish, who had quietly and for reasons long forgotten lighted candles at certain times at altars in their houses, realize they were Jewish—products of the great anti-Semitic wave that, around the time of Columbus, swept the Jews from Spain, many finding their way across the ocean to the colony of New Spain.

Below the "aristocratic" lineages were people called *mestizos*, admixtures of Spanish and Mexican Indian blood which, in fact, most of the descendants of the conquistadors were, and *coyotes*, the offspring of Spanish and New Mexican Indians. *Mulattos* were the product of Spanish and black unions, the blacks having been imported early into Mexico as laborers. In addition to these were people who came to be called *genizaros*—usually enslaved children from the nomadic tribes who were brought up in the ways of the Spanish and freed as adults. Neither Spanish nor members of any local tribe, they formed a large part of the population, an underclass whose livelihood came from laboring on behalf of others. Groups of genizaros, as well as mestizo clans, were encouraged by the award of land grants to form their own villages on the outskirts of the Spanish domain as buffers against raiding nomadic tribes. Such was the origin of several towns in the mid-1700s, including Las Truchas in the Sangre de Cristo Mountains between Taos and Santa Fe.

As Spanish dreams of conquest and the conversion of souls began to fade, the Franciscans' occasional visits to perform important sacraments such as baptisms and marriages became rare. Increasingly, the deeply, almost morbidly pious colonists were left to their own devices.

By 1798, exactly 200 years after Oñate's entrada, the secularization of the churches of New Mexico began. The Franciscans were replaced over the next two decades by a handful of priests not attached to any monastic order. Much as peculiar life-forms such as flightless birds evolve in the isolation of islands, the New Mexican colonists developed their own ways of fulfilling their spiritual needs.

*I*T IS SAID that the Spanish soul holds a deep respect for penitence in any form, and in the insular world of the mountainous villages of New Mexico, penitence took on a new form all its own. This was the *Hermanos de Nuestro Padre Jesus Nazareno*, the Brotherhood of Our Father Jesus the Nazarene, also known as the *Penitentes*, around which a great deal of ominous rumor has swirled ever since. In small church buildings or meeting houses called *moradas*, the Penitentes kept alive the feast days and other ceremonies of the Catholic calendar, with a particular intensity erupting during Holy Week.

Here, the passion of Christ was acted out in a new and dolorous liturgy made up chiefly of sorrowful hymns. It culminated in a procession to a nearby hill with an appointed brother hauling his cross while the others whipped themselves bloody with knotted cords. On the hill, the town's Calvary, the suffering brother would be tied to the cross, and he would remain there until he fainted. There is little evidence that these surrogates ever actually died on their crosses, but tales of an occasional death added to the brotherhood's mystical appeal. To the dismay of the Church's few representatives, disapproval only succeeded in driving the Penitentes to greater secrecy in their mountain villages.

Besides performing such rituals, the brotherhood took care of funerals, succored the sick and bereaved, and generally sought to act with the selflessness of Christ. Equally important, they solidified the cultural pride of the villagers. Before the end of the 19th century, the Penitentes could be found in most Hispanic villages in the colony.

What might be perceived as a sunnier side of Spanish Catholicism also arose early in the 19th century. North of Santa Fe at the headwaters of the Santa Cruz River, the Tewa Indians had long visited a small pit of dust that was believed to have strong healing powers. The place was called Tsimayo, and a local named Bernardo Abeyta asked the bishop for permission to build a chapel at the site of the pit. This became the Santuario of Chimayo, and a place where all New Mexicans could worship—the Pueblo people, the genizaros, and the Hispanics. To this day, people in the thousands make Easter Week pilgrimages on foot from as far as hundreds of miles to the santuario, partaking of the healing sand and leaving behind crutches and other offerings.

SUDDENLY, in 1821, all New Mexicans—Indian, españole, genizaro—were taken as one kind of person: citizens. That year, the people of New Spain overthrew the Spanish and declared the existence of the Republic of Mexico. The more liberal tendencies of this new government were felt quite soon in the north. While the legal equality of citizenship did little to eliminate the social distinctions people in New Mexico held dear, the Mexican government welcomed the arrival of a strange breed of foreigners—mountain men and traders, both French and American. They had already begun to appear on the horizon, and in 1821 they opened up the Santa Fe Trail, pressing their mercantile interests south into Chihuahua along the ever-perilous Camino Real, the Royal Road of the Spanish.

Some of the elite New Mexican families, the *ricos*, took on similar mercantile interests; many of the rough and charismatic newcomers intermarried and stayed. The first printing press in New Mexico arrived in 1834. Money transactions, as opposed to barter, became more common. Change was coming—slowly but certainly—at least to the less isolated parts of the province.

But still, New Mexico was no prize, its governorship a burden rather than a grand opportunity. The governors sent up from the still chaotic world of revolutionary Mexico proved even less capable than their imperial predecessors when it came to controlling the "wild" tribes, the *indios barbaros*. While the Hispanic population grew, reaching 65,000 in the 1840s, and extending east and south along the Pecos River and north into the San Luis Valley of present-day Colorado, the depredations of raiding tribes increased. Except for a lucky few, mostly centered in Santa Fe, life continued to be hard, insular, and increasingly dangerous.

Then, a mere 25 years after the new banner of the Republic of Mexico was raised over the capital at Santa Fe, it was taken down, the hapless victim of an American dream called Manifest Destiny.

IN 1978, Maria Rubio (opposite, right) of Lake Arthur, New Mexico, gained fame when she baked a tortilla that bore a likeness of the face of Jesus. Ten years later, her neighbor, Eduvijen Guillen, had the same remarkable experience.

EDWARD TRUJILLO of Guadalupe, New Mexico, holds a framed photograph in which

he is held by his grandfather. His great grandfather built the church in 1890.

*A S*ANTE F*E* TRADITION, *the enormous figure of Zozobra appears
each autumn, standing some 50 feet high, his head and arms making threatening
gestures as he growls and roars. He is said to embody the evils and sorrows
of the year past, and when he goes up in flames and perishes,
so will they. In a similar tradition, Hopi Indians gather at winter solstice
and wish the year's ills into turkey feathers, which are hung on
bushes until the icy winds of winter blow them away.*

THE MISSION *San Xavier del Bac rises in baroque splendor south of Tucson,*

Arizona. Since the late 1700s the church has served local Indian populations.

AN ADVENTUROUS
BREED

AS RAILROAD lines stretched across the Southwest in the 1880s, they brought a
multitude of goods, visitors, and new ways into the region. The narrow-gauge Cumbres & Toltec
Railway still takes passengers to high-country vistas along the New Mexico-Colorado border.

AS EARLY SNOW falls in southern Colorado, a rancher hastens to drive his cattle down from their upper pasturage, where they have spent the all-too-brief summer.

A GAP IN THE TOWERING RIM of Stonewall Valley in Colorado provided travelers

on the Santa Fe Trail with what one called a gateway "to let us into the Garden."

As TRADERS brought textiles and clothes, medicines, books, hardware, and new ideas into the Southwest, the traditional, even hidebound society of New Mexico began to shift its attention and dependence from south to north. The standard of living in the old province began to improve markedly, especially of course among the rich, many of whom entered the mercantile trade themselves. The new Hispanic merchants relied on Missouri traders, whose huge wagons were moving fortresses that tended to deter attacks by Apache along the trail south into Chihuahua. Meanwhile, Mexican bullion—chiefly silver—was flowing back into Missouri.

In 1845 the United States annexed the independent (but once Mexican) state of Texas, and soon enough a shooting skirmish there gave President James Polk a pretext for declaring war on Mexico. Colonel Stephen W. Kearny was dispatched with the grandiosely named 2,700-man Army of the West to take possession of New Mexico, Chihuahua, and California.

Many New Mexicans were predisposed by the increased prosperity of recent years to welcome American rule, but one not likely to take kindly to it was the governor of the province, Manuel Armijo, who had earlier succeeded in fending off an attack by land-hungry Texans and fancied himself a fine general. To circumvent any unpleasantness, a presidential envoy was sent into Santa Fe ahead of the army and there met privately with the governor, persuading him (probably with a bribe) to disband a group of volunteers he had assembled and flee.

Thus a major piece in the grand continental jigsaw puzzle of American Manifest Destiny was put into place. Some conjured visions of railroads tying the trans-Mississippi west to California, where one of the richest gold rushes in memory was getting under way. But the railroads would be a while in coming. For there were those, too, who pointed out that the U.S. might have bitten off in this strange desertland of New Mexico a great deal more trouble than it could readily chew. Here was poverty, illiteracy, a people who had a reputation among Americans for being backward and lazy and given to barbarous pastimes such as bullfights and cockfights. Also, anti-Catholic sentiment in the "States" was on the rise, and there was the matter of slavery: Would the new territory be free or slave?

Many New Mexicans found the newly arriving Americans as barbarous as the mountain men who had preceded them—those outlandish and devil-may-care men who had used Taos as a home base in their search for beaver pelts and were famous for brewing and consuming prodigious amounts of an alcoholic drink called Taos Lightning. Culture clash was inevitable, and it was ameliorated only because so many American merchants had married into New Mexican society and had taken leadership roles in the new polity. The Treaty of

JOHN WESLEY POWELL'S men counted echoes at a place now called Echo Park. The Green and Yampa Rivers meet serenely here, belying the rapids ahead that almost scuttled the first expedition of men through the Grand Canyon in 1869.

Guadalupe Hidalgo, which ended the Mexican-American War in 1848, had promised to honor such matters as the old Spanish land grants establishing so many Hispanic holdings. But it would be, in some measure, a deep-seated suspicion, even bigotry, toward Hispanics that would keep New Mexico from achieving statehood until the next century.

The treaty also guaranteed those land grants awarded by Spain to the Pueblo people, who were clearly altogether different from the wild, marauding tribes. Being settled agrarians, the Pueblo people were considered 'barbarians'; the others were 'savages'—terms that were commonly used for decades. But U.S. policy was such that no Indian, not even the peaceful Pueblo, could be citizens. So with the coming of the Stars and Stripes, the Pueblo lost the status of citizenship they had so briefly held under Mexico and were placed in a new limbo that would continue until the 20th century.

Meanwhile, in 1853, James Gadsden negotiated the purchase of a narrow but important strip of desertland in the southern part of the territory of New Mexico. The Gadsden Purchase was to be the last piece of Manifest Destiny. By now, an increasingly large military presence was preoccupied with defending the people of New Mexico against the likes of Navajo and Apache, who soon found that the Americans, though they had defeated the Indians' Mexican enemies, were not to be taken as newfound friends.

This was not a pretty time in history: No group in the Southwest acted with the regard for their fellowman that today we like to imagine governs our society. The chief difference, however, between human relations now and then is that today they tend to be governed by a legal system that can usually enforce order. In the Southwest before and even decades after it became part of the United States, enforcing anyone's law was a far less practical affair.

*I*N THE CENTURY before the American takeover, many Navajo had found a new material wealth centered on raising sheep (introduced by the Spanish). They had expanded their territory to the south and west, the north being out of the question thanks to the hostility of the Ute. Some Navajo increased their raiding, not just for the economic sport of it, but to fight off growing encroachment of their land by Hispanic and then white settlers, and also to recover Navajo women and children who had been taken as slaves. Both the Spanish and then the Americans would sign treaties of peace with the Navajo from time to time, assuming that the Navajo leader with whom they dealt spoke for all Navajo. But of course, in the Apachean way, no one spoke for all. A band, usually a wealthy one, might sue for peace, while another would go forth seeking vengeance, so it appeared to the European mind that solemn treaties between a sovereign white government and what they supposed was a sovereign Navajo leader, a chief, were always broken. Meanwhile, peaceful Navajo bands were punished for the transgressions of other bands, leading to the sure knowledge that white men could not be trusted.

To bring order out of this chaos, the American war department alternately sought peace and then military subjugation. Forts were established, such as Fort Defiance in northeastern Arizona (still part of the New Mexico Territory), and matters continued to deteriorate until 1860, when the Navajo, banding together in unprecedented unity, attacked Fort Defiance some 2,000-strong. Finally, after nearly succeeding, they suffered major losses from the Army's artillery and were driven off. Despite their defeat, it appeared that the Navajo had somehow won, for soon the blue-shirted troops abandoned Fort Defiance and other forts throughout the region.

The Navajo were of course unaware that the American troops had been summoned elsewhere to settle a more pressing matter—the Civil War. In the Southwest at least, a few battles, particularly in the open lands south of Santa Fe, settled the matter territorially in favor of the Union and dashed rebel dreams of a far western component for the Confederacy. Meanwhile the Navajo, and the Apache elsewhere, had undertaken even greater raiding largely undeterred. In 1862, a large column of Union troops arrived in Santa Fe from California under the generalship of James Carleton, whose orders were to settle the Civil War locally (which already had been done) and to put an end to the raiding by savages.

Carleton hired former mountain man and scout, Kit Carson, then in semi-retirement in Taos, to lead U.S. forces in a campaign to round up the raiders and put them in a 40-square-mile camp called Bosque Redondo (Round Woods) along the Pecos River. There they would be converted into Christian farmers, no matter how many generations it took. Carson first rounded up the Mescalero Apache to the south (about 400 warriors and their families), before going after the Navajo.

In two campaigns over 1866-67, he brought the Navajo to their knees, chiefly by destroying their orchards and flocks of sheep and chasing the holdouts into the dead end of Canyon de Chelly. In all, some 8,000 Navajo were rounded up and forced to walk the 300 miles to Bosque Redondo. Along the way, resident New Mexicans picked off laggards, taking them away as slaves, while the soldiers looked on. Some stragglers were evidently shot, including one woman who paused along the way to have a baby. At the end of what was called The Long Walk, the Navajo were crammed into a disease-ridden camp for four years, where many of them died.

Not long after the end of the Civil War, Carleton's policy was discredited as cruel, ineffective, and also too expensive. Furthermore, settlers in the immediate area despised the idea of Navajo in their neighborhood. The remaining Navajo, numbering some 6,000, were marched back to a reservation in northern New Mexico, given some livestock to get started again, and promised that the U.S. would provide health and education services. The Navajo had lost their stomach for warfare and violence, but the awful experience in captivity had inadvertently brought about a sense of tribal belonging among these formerly loosely associated bands. It planted the seeds of what would become today's Navajo Nation, inhabiting the largest Indian reservation in the United States (in an area about the size of West Virginia) with the largest resident population (some 250,000). Despite continuing vicissitudes, ranging from *(Continued on page 134)*

FOR 29 YEARS, beginning in 1851, troops from Fort Union (above)
in New Mexico protected commerce along the Santa Fe Trail.
The quartermaster depot (opposite, background) served as the main supply
distribution center for the U.S. Army in the Southwest.
Guns, boots, saddles, horse medicines, and other goods from the East
passed through here, but more importantly, the army's demand for supplies
helped bring about a change in the local economy from subsistence to cash,
as settlers grew corn and wheat to fill the Army's demand for forage and flour.
During the Civil War, fearing an attack by Confederate troops,
federal officers built the "star fort," (opposite, foreground) an earthen
fortification around which old trail ruts can still be seen. Troops from Fort Union
met the Confederates at Glorieta to the south. The battle was indecisive,
but the bluecoats destroyed the Southerners' supplies, forcing their withdrawal
from the Southwest. The fort was closed in 1891.

*A LONE APACHE draws a bead on an approaching wagon in
this etching by Frederic Remington (opposite). The southwestern landscape
was littered with bullets (opposite, below) and reddened with
blood as Apache and other tribes sought to protect their lands against
the juggernaut of settlers and troops. Few fallen warriors
were memorialized in the manner of John Giddings, a stagecoach
passenger who died in an Apache attack in Arizona (below).*

ON HIS SECOND Grand Canyon trip,
John Wesley Powell camped at
Little Hole, near Flaming Gorge
on Utah's Green River,
and was photographed there
by E. O. Beaman in 1871 (above).
The scene, including the stately pines
Powell wrote of, looked
much the same in 1993, when this
photograph was taken (left).

TODAY at Horn Creek Rapids on the Colorado River, the boats are smaller, but the

churning waters are just as challenging as they were in John Wesley Powell's time.

(Continued from page 125) drought to human misunderstanding, Navajo ways—their elaborate ceremonial life, their pastoral economy—would remain solidly intact for generations. General Carleton would probably, today, be appalled.

*I*N THE REMOTE and slow-to-change world of the Southwest, life was now changing at a dizzying pace. Two years before the outbreak of the Civil War, the Butterfield Overland Mail Company opened a stage line that originated in Tipton, Missouri, and snaked its way 2,800 miles to San Francisco, dipping south through El Paso, west to Tucson and Los Angeles—a route called the Ox-bow. A passenger paid $200 for the bruising 26-day trip. The effect on Tucson, a major stop along the route, was immediate. It brought a new prosperity to local merchants serving California-bound passengers, and to the people in wagon trains that followed. Tucson was soon on its way to becoming the largest town in Arizona.

The Butterfield route passed directly through the territory of the Chiricahua Apache, east of Tucson, then led by the most famous of all of the Chiricahua's charismatic leaders, Cochise. This tall, eagle-eyed Apache vowed not to disturb the stage line but remained suspicious of the influx of white men. Finally, in a misunderstanding with a hotheaded young officer named Bascom who accused Cochise (probably falsely) of treachery, full-scale mayhem broke out. Overland travel became all the more perilous, with numerous drivers and passengers killed. Even so, the stage line missed its tight schedule only once in its entire history.

In the north, in the land of the Paiute, Mormon settlers began to appear, bringing with them a communal kind of agriculture perfectly suited to these arid lands, learned in the Promised Land around Salt Lake and based on precepts set down in gold tablets years earlier in upstate New York. Before long, the Paiute were working as day laborers on Mormon farms, their ancient desert culture nearly obliterated.

In the early 1860s, just as Arizona split off from New Mexico to become its own territory, the last of the mountain men changed Arizona history. Joseph Walker is today considered one of the greatest of these trappers and adventurers who, in their quest for beaver, had created the first maps of the vast wilderness that lay between the western plains and California. Walker had discovered a pass across the Sierra Nevada, and a river and lake were named for him as well. Along the Hassayampa River in the Bradshaw Mountains of central Arizona, Walker and other prospectors found placer gold. They also found primary deposits in the hills near a stream they named Lynx Creek, after one of the men picked up a dead lynx along its bank and discovered, to his extreme pain, that it was still alive.

Miners soon flooded into this region previously unknown to whites, and soldiers followed to protect these newfound interests. Like dandelions, mining towns grew up—in canyons along streams, and on the nearly vertical faces of high mountains. Places like Prescott, Jerome, and Wickenburg came into being, along with others like Walker, Bumble Bee, and Vulture that later faded into ghost towns or merely road signs along remote Forest Service roads. The town of Prescott would boom long enough to become the capital of the Territory of Arizona, which split off from New Mexico in 1863, and eventually become a thriving center whose streets were adorned with the finest in Eastern-style Victorian architecture.

But before such grandeur was even imaginable, and as freebooting prospectors and mining toughs were swarming the mountains and many other locales in the Southwest, a new industry sprang up as well. The soldiers, as well as the miners and retailers of various camp-following services in the boomtowns, needed to be supplied with food—beef—and cattlemen soon appeared to fill this vacuum. The need became all the greater when the soldiers under Gen. George Crook succeeded in the 1870s in defeating the wild tribes of the mountains and placing them on reservations: more mouths the U.S. government was obliged to feed. Such contracts were increasingly lucrative, and men would feud and fight over them throughout much of the Southwest, during the few largely lawless decades that established in the American mind its principal mythological character, the cowboy-gunfighter.

Within a few years after the Civil War, there were essentially no places on the map of the United States labeled "unknown," with one major exception: the interior of the Grand Canyon, that definitive icon of the American Southwest. In 1869, this last unexplored piece was challenged by a tenacious preacher's son and self-taught naturalist who, as a Union officer, had lost his right arm to a Confederate ball in the battle of Shiloh: John Wesley Powell. He led a ten-man, four-boat expedition that set off on May 24, 1869, from Green River, Wyoming Territory. More than three months and almost a thousand miles later, Powell put ashore at Grand Wash Cliffs at the southern extreme of the Grand Canyon, where the Colorado River ceases its mad rush through the world's greatest chasm and settles into a stately journey to the Gulf of California. Thought to have perished along the way, Powell emerged a major hero. His account of the voyage published six years later, *Exploration of the Colorado River of the West and Its Tributaries*, became something of a best-seller. River guides quote the Tennyson-like passages to clients to this day.

Powell would leverage his heroic journey into an astonishing career as an explorer, scientist, and public servant, organizing several scientific expeditions through the high desert country of Utah and lands south. In the course of these trips, he established that the great canyonlands of the Southwest had been created not suddenly by some catastrophic event, but by the steady process of erosion through the eons. This put the final nail in the coffin of a semireligious geological theory called catastrophism that had prevailed for centuries, and ushered in the modern age of geological thinking.

Powell also was perhaps the most important Cassandra in the history of the opening of the West, which included the arid and semiarid lands west of the 100th meridian. He noted early on that the prevailing dogma—"rain follows the plow"— was a myth. By the 1870s, the West was being carved into sections of 640 acres, where homesteaders were encouraged to settle and farm, a system that was already turning the moister midwest into one of the world's great agricultural regions. Powell produced a revolutionary work in 1878 titled, awkwardly, *Report on the Lands of the Arid Region of the United States, With a More Detailed Account of the Lands of Utah, With Maps.* In it, he pointed out that in such country a farmer needed, and could handle, only half a section, so rich were western soils if irrigated. He also pointed out that ranching required several sections, and that ranching should only be done cooperatively with large commons around a small community of ranch homes, much like the cooperative Mormon settlements he had observed in Utah.

His most revolutionary notion, so revolutionary he himself put it in italics, was this: *The right to use water should inhere in the land to be irrigated, and water rights should go with land titles.* The system already at work was based on British riparian law wherein whoever controls a spring effectively controls all the land around or downstream. This was already leading to local monopolies by landowners or hastily contrived water companies. No single arid-region farmer, he noted, could afford the kinds of earthworks, stream diversions, and other irrigation projects needed, so he urged a law that would permit cooperatives and offer government assistance for such projects. So much for the myth of the rugged individualist of the West.

Powell's report, published at a time of unusually heavy rains in the West, went unheeded. Within years the homesteading process had led to countless failures, and the rapid consolidation of failed claims into vast landholdings that came to be held, for the most part, by absentee owners in the East and abroad. The accumulation of such holdings, though achieved by different means, would become a defining characteristic of the lands of the Southwest, and would provide the region with some of its most tawdry and most famous doings.

Shortly after the Civil War, a group of lawyers and businessmen, both Anglo and Hispanic, marched with great skill and cunning into the bog of New Mexico land grants. These were often vaguely defined but usually vast tracts of land awarded by the Spanish king and several Mexican governors over the centuries to Hispanic families, whole communities, and to Pueblo tribes. The group, known as the Santa Fe Ring, dominated the emerging economy and the politics of New Mexico for some 30 years, chiefly by laying its hands on most of the large land grants—by purchase, legal manipulation, and outright fraud—selling some off to investors as far away as England and keeping some for themselves.

The Ring's tentacles embraced Democrats and Republicans, civil servants and territorial legislators, businessmen, and a few governors. Once they had absorbed all the land they could, they proceeded to make further fortunes in mining, railroads, and ranching, a great deal of which took place on land they controlled. Most of this was accomplished with legal chicanery, rubber surveys, and bizarre rumor mongering. And of course there was violence. The Ring quietly took sides in a dispute that arose in Lincoln County, which then equalled approximately one-fourth of New Mexico. It involved a Texas cattleman named John Chisum who had moved his huge operation into New Mexico, as well as a storekeeper in the town of Lincoln who found himself in competition with an enterprising English merchant to supply the local army post at Fort Stanton.

Each side of the mercantile dispute in a sense suborned its own local lawman, and gangs were soon going at each other. Sporadic killings and vengeance turned into the Lincoln County War of the late 1870s, in which a teenage sociopath named Henry McCarty, then William Antrim, then Billy Bonney, rose to a fame largely unjustified by the facts of his brief career. Before he was killed at age 21, Billy the Kid had been dubbed the most lethal gunman ever known in the West.

Exaggerated reports designed to feed the fascination of the East with the Wild West claimed at Billy's death that he had killed at least one man for each of his 21 years—perhaps 50 in all. In fact, he killed four men and participated in a few gun-fights that resulted in a handful of other deaths. Yet, upon his death at the hands of Lincoln County sheriff Pat Garrett, a New York newspaper intoned that he "had built up a criminal organization worthy of the underworld of any of the European capitals ... he became, in the short span of his twenty-one years, the master criminal of the American southwest."

Of course, the locals did their part to spread the myth of the Southwest, as well. One poem of the time, in the old western style of making oneself seem greater for putting up with grievous hardship, tells how the Devil came upon southern Arizona and proceeded to stud "the land with the prickly pears / and scattered the cactus everywhere." He went on to import Apache, rattlesnakes, and skunks, to poison local waters with alkali, and fix the heat at one hundred and seven degrees.

> And after he fixed things so thorny and well,
> He said: 'I'll be damned if that don't beat hell.'
> ...And now, no doubt, in some corner of hell
> He gloats over the work he has done so well,
> And vows that Arizona cannot be beat
> For scorpions, tarantulas, snakes and heat.

This story of Arizona, "The Land That God Forgot," was written in 1879 by Charles O. Brown, a Tucson bartender.

Before long, Tucson would be eclipsed by what may be the greatest fast-forward, boom-and-bust town in the history of the nation, a place called Tombstone. In 1877, a strange figure appeared in the neighborhood: a tall, gaunt man with long hair and matted beard, wearing clothes patched with rabbit skins. This was Edward Schieffe-lin, a lone and fanatical prospector who began roaming the low hills east of the San Pedro River and a few miles southwest of Cochise's former stronghold in the crags of the Dragoon Mountains. Soldiers at nearby Fort Huachuca told him that the only rock he would find there would be his own tombstone, so that is the name given to the town that erupted once Schieffelin found rich veins of silver in the hills.

By the time bartender Brown wrote his ode, people had flocked to Tombstone from as far away as England, and the population was about 1,500 souls. Most of these frantically scoured the countryside to lay further claims beyond the 17 mines Schieffelin found and subsequently sold. By 1880 the Southern Pacific Railroad

A YOUNG COWBOY finds another practical use for the local car wash in Pecos, Texas (opposite). Pecos claims to be the site of the first rodeo, a competition among three teenage cowboys in 1883. The only major sport to arise directly from the actual tasks of laboring men, rodeo still engages the youth of the Southwest (below, right). Since the first paid-attendance rodeo took place in Prescott, Arizona, in 1888, countless contestants have suffered the fate of this bronc rider in Cimarron, New Mexico (below, left).

CAREFUL MAINTENANCE of the steam engine of the Cumbres & Toltec Scenic Railway

enables North America's highest narrow-gauge train to get over the 10,000-foot Chama Pass.

*NEWT KEEN, proprietor of Keen's Restaurant in Mentone, Texas, demonstrates
a well-accepted rule of western etiquette: Gentlemen do not need to remove their hats
indoors. Only newcomers, greenhorns, and carpetbaggers go hatless.*

tracks had passed north of the new boomtown, and reached Tucson amid "a grand
jollification," giving that city a needed economic jolt. By the beginning of 1881,
Tombstone was the largest city in the Arizona Territory, with more than 4,000 citizens, 600 houses, two churches, and a school. Mills and smelters sprang up, as
well as dance halls, brothels, saloons, and gambling dens. The town and its surrounding area was soon infested by thieves given to holding up stagecoaches and
the trains carrying silver out and all manner of supplies in.

Miners unionized and struck for a pay raise from three to four dollars a day. In
response, the mines were closed for four months until the men went back to work
at the old rate. By 1886, mines began to shut down—lower prices for silver and the
expense of pumping out water were making for profitless work—and by the end of
the decade, silver mining continued only sporadically. The flourishing city of Tombstone began heading for ghost status. At the turn of the century, a few local mines
were producing manganese, and the glory days were long gone. The town that had
hosted the Earp Brothers and the gunfight at OK Corral, along with a thriving saloon
and gambling business, a booming red-light district, and a sizable array of homes
for polite society, was little more than a husk.

When the oddball Ed Schieffelin arrived in the Tombstone area, no other

Americans were to be found between the San Pedro River and the lands lying west of the Rio Grande. This was all Chiricahua Apache country. By the time the bell began to toll in earnest for the boosters in Tombstone, the Apache were gone.

Under the generalship of George Crook, who had earlier cleared the Arizona highlands of Yavapai and Apache and subsequently went off to campaign in the north, most of the Chiricahua Apache were successfully rounded up and placed on a reservation called San Carlos, north of their ancestral lands, jammed in with other Apache for whom they had only distaste. Among these was a man called Goyahkla, also known as Geronimo. A fierce and brilliant warrior, he broke out of San Carlos several times in a desperate attempt not so much to escape the Americans as to inflict as much vengeance upon them as he could before the inevitable end.

Chiricahua were capable of nearly superhuman feats—easily traveling up to 60 miles a day over the desert and rangeland, finding water where it seemed utterly absent, disappearing in a trice into the landscape. At the same time, General Crook was an implacable and highly respected adversary. He had adopted unusual tactics such as using mules rather than horses (mules had more stamina in difficult terrain) and relying on the use of Chiricahua scouts. Such unusual ways made Crook's superiors in the Department of War nervous.

Geronimo's final breakout in late 1885 led to the replacement of General Crook with General Nelson Miles, and by mid-1886 some 5,000 troops were in the field, approximately one-quarter of the standing army of the United States, seeking to run down Geronimo and his band of 34, including women and children. Finally, in September of that year, Geronimo appeared in a place on the Arizona-New Mexico border called Skeleton Canyon to surrender, having received from Miles a promise that after a few years' incarceration in far-off Florida, he would be returned to his people. For all intents and purposes, the last of the Indian Wars was over in the United States. Henceforth, the only violence from that quarter would be outbreaks from the reservations such as Wounded Knee.

But under orders from President Grover Cleveland, Miles broke his word. He sent Geronimo and the few renegades, along with all the other Chiricahua from the San Carlos Reservation and even those who had served the U.S. Army as scouts, to what amounted to two concentration camps in Florida. There, crowding, disease, ennui, and a wholly different climate and landscape would cause many to die. For 27 years, the entire group known as the Chiricahua would languish as prisoners of war in Florida, Alabama, and finally Oklahoma. By 1913, some 80 would remain as private landholders in Oklahoma, while about 170 would choose to live with the Mescalero on their reservation in New Mexico. Today, many still proudly trace their lineage back to people like Geronimo, but there is no longer any social entity known as Chiricahua.

In the Southwest, order and a kind of peace would soon reign. A spiderweb of narrow-gauge tracks was painfully spun throughout the precipitous cliffs and gorges of the southern Rockies in Colorado to bring silver and other ore north and south to shipping points. As rails stretched over the landscape, they brought a new pariah class to the Southwest in the form of Chinese laborers, just as the mining camps attracted enclaves of Europeans.

Mormon farmers continued to move southward into Arizona, irrigating farms with water from the Salt, Gila, and other rivers—and incidentally draining it away from Pima Indian farmers who had earlier helped supply the army and the settlers with grain. The Pima fell into penury, as did the Papago and the Apache of both Arizona and New Mexico, where many of the tribal people sought a living by running cattle or working in the white man's mines and on his farms. In Arizona, copper was king, the territory becoming the largest producer of this metal so crucial as the nation electrified. But cattle were also important to the economics of the region. Men like Californian George Hearst (father of the newspaperman-to-be, William Randolph Hearst) began amassing unimaginably vast tracts of land into ranch holdings: Hearst's Diamond A property in the Southwest amounted to a piece about the size of a small New England state.

More and more, the relatively lush but fragile grasslands of the deserts and the lands to the north would soon give way to woody scrub, even oceans of sagebrush, as cattle companies bent on maximizing profits began to overgraze the land. Similarly, in the north on the large part of the Colorado Plateau that comprised the Navajo Reservation, the sheep had begun to overgraze the land as well.

*W*ITH THE RAILROADS came tourists, travelers seeking a glimpse of the storied landscapes and lifestyles of the Southwest: the Spanish haciendas, the hard-bitten and colorful cowboys, and of course the Indians, now variously seen as quaint or noble, and certainly soon to disappear. Hotels arose in cow towns along the railroad tracks, and hardy travelers took buggies into such remote and roadless places as the Hopi mesas, there to watch in fascination as snake priests danced in the plazas in late August with vipers in their mouths, all to bring rain to their ancient cornfields in the desertlands below.

The tourists, in turn, were a market for Indian goods, chiefly craft items, and trains pausing in places such as Albuquerque were greeted by the exotic sight of pueblo women in shawls with pottery for sale. A number of Anglos and Hispanics took up the life of traders on Indian reservations, acting as catalysts for the production and sale of such items as Navajo rugs and serving as a kind of bank, barter, and pawn system that joined the Indians, however tenuously, with the cash economy of the outside world. Navajo, ever adaptable, had taken up the making of silver and turquoise jewelry, chiefly for their own purposes. Soon a market began to open up for Navajo jewelry and then the more delicate Zuni pieces.

The market for Indian crafts grew rapidly after the turn of the century, and soon unwary tourists were buying commercial geegaws made by Indians in what amounted to sweatshops. Old tribal crafts—pottery and basketry, for example—were becoming lost arts among some tribes due to the availability of cheap substitutes such as metal pots and pans. Authentic examples were sought after by anthropologists, museums, and private collectors, and soon, in the early decades of the 20th century, organized revivals of old Indian crafts would begin in earnest.

After the turn of the century, the national movement toward preservation reached even the remote and little known lands of the Southwest—thanks largely to that early conservationist and Old West fan, Theodore Roosevelt. Armed with the Antiquities Act, he began declaring some of the more astonishing landscapes of the country to be national monuments and national parks. By 1908 such places as the ruins at Mesa Verde, the petrified forest remnants near Holbrook, and the Grand Canyon had come under federal protection. Meanwhile national forests were growing in area (often land that had been manipulated out of the hands of early land grant owners was profitably sold to the Forest Service). Soon enough a permit system gave ranchers long-term licenses to graze these public lands and logging companies comfortable leases for timbering. Conservation of natural resources, in those days and especially in the West where the world was young, vast, and apparently renewable, meant using them. Why let trees rot in place? Why let a river's water flow uselessly by only to enter some distant gulf?

In 1911 the federal government built a huge dam across the Salt River east of Phoenix, the better to make use of those waters, and named it for Teddy Roosevelt. The flatlands downstream became a major cotton-producing region, and the small settlement of Phoenix was on its way to becoming the Southwest's largest city by far. The desert indeed could be made to bloom. Soon enough even the mighty Colorado would be similarly dammed, its grand torrent tamed to produce power and to be sold off by the millions of acre feet to support cities, ranches, and farms throughout the Southwest, and to water California's Imperial Valley, turning that no-man's-land into one of the richest agricultural engines on the planet.

Meanwhile, another kind of energy was about to be unleashed in the older settlements of northern New Mexico, in particular Santa Fe and the town of Taos, once a haven for mountain men and the scene of the grandest remaining example of native architecture, the Pueblo of Taos.

After New Mexico achieved statehood in 1912, some leaders in Santa Fe noted that their city was a haphazard mixture of old-style adobe buildings and more modern brick structures common throughout much of the United States—in effect, a place without much by way of an identity, and therefore a hard sell to tourists. Led by the staff of the Museum of Santa Fe and impelled by equal parts of scholarship, sentiment, and boosterism, the city began a program of self-transformation. From pueblo architecture like that at Taos and from old Spanish mission churches and haciendas, they created a new style of building called variously Santa Fe style, New Mexican Mission, or Pueblo-Hispanic. Among the elements were thick stucco walls over adobe brick, Spanish porches called portals that softened the blocky appearance of real pueblo buildings, and exposed cross-beams supporting ceilings. Corners, doorways, and niches in walls all bore the work of the handmade—exactly straight lines were eschewed. Spanish-style corner fireplaces were renamed kiva fireplaces, the Indian word being, it was thought, more salable. Civic buildings and residences were built in this new style.

Embodied in the new architecture—something old, something new, and something borrowed—was in part the reality and in greater part the ideal notion of the three cultures—Hispanic, Indian, and Anglo—happily wedded. It was bruited in national magazines as "a true product of America." This would, indeed, become the signature building style of the state of New Mexico, and it is considered the signature style of the Southwest by most people.

In Santa Fe, they built it and the people came—notably artists and other intellectuals, and the hoped-for tourists. Many sought a purer, more organic way of life; others would find that the extreme aridity was good for their lungs.

Among those seeking to heal their souls was Mabel Dodge, who had been the famous host of the grandest, most interesting salon in New York City before the war: a hotbed of socialists, anarchists, poets, artists, lawyers, psychoanalysts, Wobblies, single-taxers, seers, and government officials. Mabel ventured to Taos, where she saw before her the blend of nature, art, and community she believed would be the redemption of America. There she settled, building a house that was a cross between Santa Fe style and a Florentine mansion. She married a Taos Pueblo Indian named Tony Luhan, and began to invite people to share her vision, among them D. H. Lawrence. Soon Mabel was the energetic center of a thriving art colony in Taos; the Southwest was now emblazoned on the map. Writers, politicians, painters, dancers—people of all stripes arrived, many stopping off for good in Santa Fe or Taos.

Among Mabel's visitors in the 1920s was a young social worker named John Collier. He became convinced from observing pueblo life that the current notion (and policy) that assumed it would be best if Indians simply faded into the great American melting pot was wrong. Here he saw the same vibrancy that Mabel perceived, and this notion would be his guiding principle when, as the Great Depression got under way, he was appointed head of the Bureau of Indian Affairs. In 1934 Collier's ideas were embodied in the Indian Reorganization Act, which provided, among other things, that Indian tribes would have their own constitutions, setting up tribal governments based loosely on American models. Once in place, these governments would allow tribes to exercise increased sovereignty over their own affairs. This bill, with the governments that were subsequently created, is widely credited for the continued existence of American Indians in their tribal societies.

By the late 1930s, the Southwest—for all its tourists, national parks, mines, Indian tribes, artists, and ranches (both working and dude)—for all its newfound bustle, remained still a comparatively remote, unknown, and sleepy part of the United States. Much of the southwestern expanse was still served at best by unpaved roads, hardly the sort of place where one would have expected to witness the greatest single change in human history.

A STRAY white cat seems an apparition in the Arizona ghost town of Whitehouse, one of dozens of such places where dreams of riches brought American miners and ranchers swarming into the Southwest.

PROSPECTORS *eagerly brought their finds to the assay office in Vulture, Arizona (below), a town that flourished for three decades, beginning in the 1860s. In Jerome, Arizona, a hotel room with a view (opposite) looks east to the Black Hills. A copper-mining town, Jerome clings to a precipitous 30-degree slope. Since the mine closed in 1953, Jerome has reinvented itself several times, and now is home to a new crop of artists and craftsmen.*

THE AMERICAN COWBOY adopted chaps (pronounced SHAPS) from Mexican

vaqueros. *The leather coverings protect cowboys from rope burn and mesquite brush.*

LIGHTNING CRACKLES in the sky behind the Chisos Mountains in Texas'

Big Bend National Park, a stark reminder of nature's grand scale.

LAND OF MANY SUNS

*IN THE ARID AND UNCOMPROMISING LANDS of the
American Southwest, a fork in the road seems to offer two equally forbidding
choices, and helpful road signs can be few and far between.*

BULLDOG PRIDE: The high school football stadium in Artesia,

New Mexico, which holds some 10,000 fans, fills to capacity for big games.

LIKE EARTH and turquoise, the Colorado and Little Colorado Rivers meet, carrying rafters

to a sandy beach. Light reflecting from mineral particles gives the Little Colorado its hue.

THE AMERICAN SOUTHWEST comprises about 10 percent of the landmass of the United States, a mere 3 percent of its population, and by some reckoning, 6 percent of practicing non-Indian shamans. In one small village called Portal in Arizona, more than half the population holds Ph.D.'s in biology and related fields, and there may be more physicists and astronomers per capita in the Southwest than anywhere else in the world. In another southwestern town, one of the chief industries is UFOs.

In the American Southwest, the chili pepper is considered this hemisphere's greatest gift to the world, second only, perhaps, to constitutional democracy. There are more canyons here than anyone has counted (many of them secret places known only to a few) and landscapes that virtually every American has imprinted in mind. In this regard, it is difficult to recall any make of automobile that has not been advertised speeding through a southwestern backdrop or perched dramatically atop a pinnacle in Monument Valley. Visitors can still note a regional costume in the airports—people of all ethnic tints in cowboy boots and hats, ruffled skirts and turquoise. It is the only region in the country where both Indians and Hispanics are major cultural presences and political forces to be reckoned with.

In this place, many consider the sun as a living father, a deity, and here humanity first tried out its very own imitation of the sun—and in so doing changed the world, not to mention the Southwest.

No one knew exactly what would happen on the morning of July 16, 1945, out on the edge of the *malpais*, the badlands, of Jornada del Muerto. The gadget (so it was called) was mounted on a hundred-foot tower that swayed in dusty winds and suffered a series of lightning storms. The mastermind, Robert Oppenheimer, bet a dollar in the scientists' pool: When the device went off it would be the equivalent of 300 tons of TNT. Edward Teller guessed 45,000 tons. Both were wrong.

Meanwhile, Enrico Fermi, the Italian Nobelist, took wagers on whether the contrivance would ignite the atmosphere and destroy the Southwest, even the world. This wagering annoyed Maj. Gen. Leslie Groves, whose job was to see that the gadget was tested by the next day, July 17, when Franklin Delano Roosevelt, Winston Churchill, and Josef Stalin met at Potsdam to carve up the postwar world. Earlier Groves had warned the bewildered governor of New Mexico that he might need to declare martial law when the sun rose on July 16.

Distinguished visitors waited in bunkers some 20 miles away from the tower. At 05:29:45, the gadget's firing circuit closed, and in a fraction of a second, a pinprick of light became the light of a thousand suns.

The tower was vaporized, a fireball grew—looking, as one observer put it, "like a monstrous, convoluting brain." Then a massive purple cloud began to

A JEEP KICKS UP THE DUST on a dirt track in Arizona's Saguaro National Park.
The Sonoran Desert's signature feature, the saguaro cactus can
reach a height of 50 feet and live nearly 200 years.

mushroom into the sky; it flattened out at 40,000 feet into a ring of ash a mile wide. People heard the explosion a hundred miles away. Windows broke in Gallup, New Mexico, 185 miles from Ground Zero.

In an attempt to gauge the force of the explosion, Enrico Fermi released some scraps of paper into the oncoming blast wave. They were thrown some 2.5 meters which, Fermi guessed, corresponded to a blast from 10,000 tons of TNT. His estimate was low by 8,600 tons.

Later, in and around the crater where the tower had once stood, the scientists came across a substance heretofore unknown on earth. They called the greenish, jadelike material Trinitite, after the oddly sacred-sounding name they had bestowed on Ground Zero—the Trinity Site. The world had, irrevocably, entered the nuclear age.

When John Wesley Powell headed the U.S. Geological Survey in the 1880s, it was the largest and brightest assemblage of government scientists anywhere in the world. But with the astounding buildup of scientists in a remote, onetime boys' school and camp in the Jemez Mountains in New Mexico—a place called Los Alamos—and in the other labs, all devoted to the secret wartime production of the weapon to end all wars, government science was launched on a trajectory steeper than anyone had ever seen before. Soon, in addition to the gathering of physicists and technicians at Los Alamos, President Truman established the Sandia National Laboratories in nearby Albuquerque. Its responsibility would be to engineer all the components of the nation's nuclear arsenal, except the warheads.

The arrival of thousands of can-do engineers and scientists in the late 1940s changed life dramatically in Albuquerque. What was by national standards not much more than a provincial town—and sleepy to boot—began to grow into a major Western city designed for the automobile. Like others in the Southwest, Albuquerque is one of the fastest growing cities in the nation, spurred in great part by the spinning off of technology from Sandia and Los Alamos labs, now engaged as well in fields such as energy technology, supercomputing, the Human Genome Project, and even such charmingly unthreatening quests as determining, by computer simulation and acoustical physics, the sounds that were probably emitted by duck-billed dinosaurs. Though hardly a new Silicon Valley, the Southwest is home to the largest production plant of the world's largest manufacturer of computer chips: Intel, just a rifle shot outside Albuquerque's city limits.

In this place of skies so clear that one can almost see through the blue overhead into the blackness of outer space, astronomy has a special place. From the Davis Mountains in Texas in an arc that ends with Mount Hopkins, huge telescopes eye the heavens night and day, collecting pinpricks of light and infrared and gamma rays, seeking answers to how the universe works. In between, on New Mexico's Plains of San Augustin, is what is called, with a certain lack of poetry, the Very Large Array. The VLA, a collection of 27 radio telescopes, is now part of a global hookup that seeks to find, among other things, telltale signs of intelligent life elsewhere in the cosmos.

*T*HROUGHOUT THE SOUTHWEST, the postwar story was similar. Numerous war veterans, having trained in military bases that sprang up in places such as Tucson and Alamogordo, decided to stay in the region. Today, military installations make up a considerable part of the Southwest. In addition to military bases, there is the huge missile-testing range that stretches north from White Sands National Monument and the colossal strip of parched land called the Barry M. Goldwater Air Force Range, a bombing range that reaches from the western edge of Tohono O'odham country almost to Yuma on the Colorado River.

Many of the new postwar pioneers in the Southwest had trained as pilots or support crew, and it was their mode, the airplane, that also played a major role in transforming the Southwest after World War II. Soon the airlines made it possible for people—tourists as well as prospective residents, many of them retirees seeking their place in the Sunbelt—to get here in a relative trice, rather than by riding the endless distances across forbidding desertlands in uncomfortable trains or overheating automobiles.

Once they arrived, another less heralded technological advance called air-conditioning made it more likely that they would stay, especially in places such as Tucson and Phoenix and Las Cruces. In the flatlands of *(Continued on page 176)*

WELCOMING SMILES greeted thousands who came to Roswell, New Mexico, on the 50th anniversary of the most celebrated "arrival" of aliens on planet Earth. Mecca for believers in the paranormal, New Mexico also has, in Los Alamos, one of the country's greatest concentrations of physicists.

*Two cowboys take a break from the endless chores of ranching,
having driven 20 miles for a cup of coffee in Roy's Ice Cream Parlor in
Carrizozo, New Mexico (above). Not far from here, in the historic
badlands of the Jornada del Muerto, Apache once harassed the old triennial
Spanish wagon trains. It was also in the badlands that, on
July 16, 1945, the United States ushered the world into the atomic age.
Though under the gun from modern economics and
environmentalism, many of the Southwest's ranchers (opposite) refuse
to give up the old ways. A seasoned cowboy (below) relaxes with a cigarette.*

Three young cowboys hold on to Thumper, a stuffed bull forever riled, at the Eastern

New Mexico State Fair. For most, the ride is close enough to the spine-wrenching real thing.

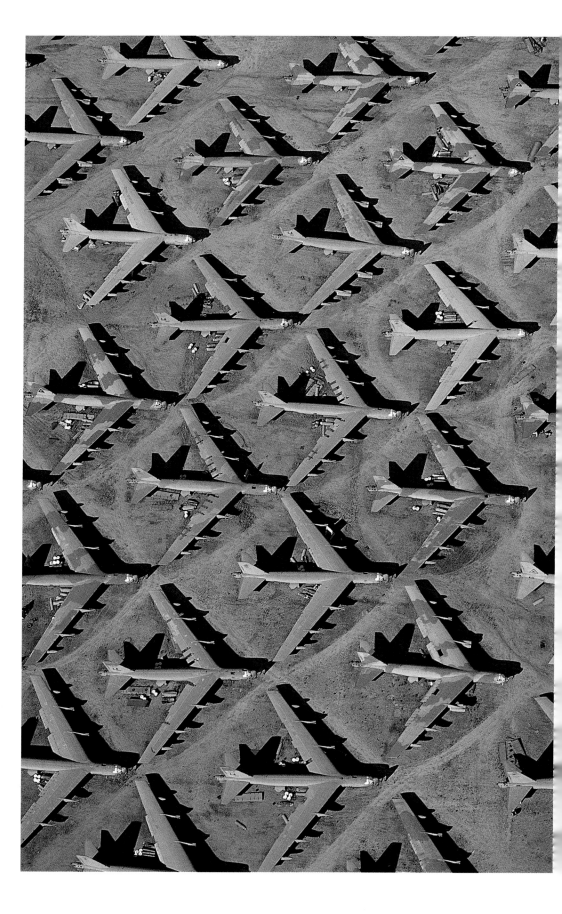

THE MILITARY, *a major presence since World War II,*
brought a vast influx of people to the Southwest, changing it from
a sleepy regional backwater to one of the fastest growing parts of the nation.
In Tucson, the Davis-Monthan Air Force Base is home
to a flock of mothballed bombers (opposite). Nestled in the sand
along southern Arizona's Devil's Highway, a practice bomb and a patch
of sand verbena (above) make a stark still life at the
Barry M. Goldwater Air Force Range.
Desert bighorn sheep, Sonoran pronghorns, and other wildlife
inhabit the military facility, which adjoins the Cabeza
Prieta National Wildlife Refuge.

HOPI BASKETRY and Navajo rugs and jewelry adorn the window of Richardson's

Trading Company in the reservation border town of Gallup, New Mexico.

PEOPLE COME *from as far as 70 miles away to "set and talk"*
and play pool at the Girvin Social Club, a saloon in Girvin, Texas,
where for 40 years customers have consumed
longnecks to the throb and wail of country-western songs.
In this comfortable meeting place, school bus seats serve as benches,
cow skulls decorate the walls, and
the wood stove burns mesquite brought
by regular customers.

Leisha Wardlaw and her father get to the church the old-style way in Alamo Village,

near Brackettville, Texas. The site was the location of several John Wayne Westerns.

(*Continued from page 163*) Phoenix, for example, surrounded with a few jagged mountains and mountain ranges but fundamentally a desertscape, the temperature can easily climb to 120 degrees in summer. At such temperatures, for obvious reasons, humans cease to be particularly ambitious or, for that matter, to move very much at all. It is much the same in summertime for most of the southern part of the Southwest. Cooling devices have long been available—simple machines that blow air cooled by evaporation down through openings in the roof. Called "swamp coolers," they are tiny "slingshots" against the monstrous heat of the Southwest summer. Boosters say that it gets very hot, but it's dry heat, and this is quite true. But most humans operate less happily at temperatures above 100 degrees, dry or humid. (In such weather the blue-woolen-clad American troops chased the more intelligently outfitted Apache a century ago—and not that effectively.)

There is a pretty continuum between the prehistoric invention of stone-lined storage pits and air conditioners that has had a profound effect on the demographics of the American Southwest. Both permitted people to live in seemingly more permanent conditions, safe from the vagaries and extremes of the climate.

As a result of these and many other factors, however, the Southwest today has become one of the most urbanized regions in the nation, in the sense of where most of the population is to be found. Six metropolitan areas in Arizona and New Mexico (Phoenix, Tucson, Flagstaff, Albuquerque, Santa Fe, and Las Cruces) account for about 60 percent of the two states' residents. Phoenix itself is the seventh largest city in the nation, one of fewer than a dozen with populations in excess of a million people. In 1900, Phoenix was a town of some 5,500 souls, while Albuquerque (now about 670,000) was slightly larger—about 6,200. These fast-growing cities and others in the region have long since found themselves wandering what may well be the murkiest corridors of Western polity: federal, state, municipal, county, local, and Indian water policy.

Early in this century, but especially during the New Deal era, the federal government was made aware that the continued welfare and growth of the West, including the Southwest, depended on increasing the availability of water. By 1936, four of the largest dams in the world were under construction on Western rivers, including the Colorado. Vast reservoirs came into being, and water churning through their hydroelectric turbines created electricity that was supposed to pay for the construction of the dams. Water was pumped to irrigate farm and ranch land. The idea at the time was to allow small farms to flourish, but there is a law of Western physics that says that water runs toward money and power. The main beneficiaries of these enormous waterworks were ever larger agricultural installations and, soon enough, the developers of the booming cities.

By the 1960s, it was becoming clear in Tucson and Phoenix, among other places, that available water from river systems, water projects, and groundwater would not be sufficient to sustain their growth, and the Central Arizona Project was conceived as a way to bring the state's fair share of the Colorado River to where the people were. Pumping water from the mile-deep Grand Canyon, for example, was beyond even the most grandiose engineering dream, but downstream the river leaves the canyonlands on its way to the Gulf of California. From Lake Havasu, north of Parker, the water could be pumped 2,900 feet up to reach the state's great population centers.

The project's gestation period was long by any standard—about three decades—and its cost in the billions of dollars, but today open-air concrete aqueducts bring water more than 300 miles across the state. The water is expensive and a bit saline, and unlike the old days of federal largesse, a far larger part of the costs must be borne by today's users.

Water conservation is the talk of the region, and a new way of obtaining water for a burgeoning population and the influx of industry has emerged: trading water rights. Very few people (including this author) understand exactly how such trading works, but the pattern is that farmers and others can rent or sell off their water rights to far-off cities and other thirsty and wealthy users. In parts of the Southwest today a silent auction is under way, the net effect of which is to take water from rural and agricultural uses and pour it into the urban areas where, of course, the majority of people are.

The situation is complicated by other considerations. Indian tribes, for example, have begun to assert their treaty and other legitimate rights to water passing

NO FRILLS SIGNS and warm hellos beckon those in search of memorable barbecue in towns across Texas. Residents of the Lone Star State and New Mexico maintain a vigorous rivalry over which state produces the best barbecue, the hottest chili peppers, and the perfect Mexican-style food. Both claim victory.

through their lands. At the same time, if anything has been constant in the history (and prehistory) of the Southwest, it is the cyclical occurrence of drought. In a drought cycle, the Colorado River, for example, could fail to produce enough water to meet all the solemnly ratified allocations of its waters to the seven states—and Mexico—that rely on it and its tributaries. It has been noted also, in irrigated systems beginning as early as ancient Mesopotamia, that irrigation tends over time to concentrate salts not just in the water but in the soil, rendering it unusable. This has begun to happen in areas heavily irrigated with water from the Colorado. Also, dams silt up, and reservoirs in arid areas evaporate a lot of water. By one estimate, Lake Mead and Lake Powell, the creations of Hoover and Glen Canyon Dams, evaporate 1.5 million acre-feet of water each year—one tenth of the Colorado River's average annual flow. More than ever, water remains the single greatest challenge in the Southwest.

*I*N ADDITION TO ALL the other kinds of urban problems any American city faces to one degree or another, some places in the Southwest face a particular problem that afflicts boomtowns. There have always been boomtowns in the Southwest, from Snaketown and Mesa Verde to the raw bustle of the old mining towns, but the ones of today face a problem widely called "Aspenization." Some of these, like the resort town of Sedona, Arizona, located amid some of the region's most spectacular red rock country, have come about almost overnight.

In the 1950s, Sedona consisted mostly of a wide street and a strip of saloon-front stores under overhanging roofs and a couple of third-generation traders of Indian crafts. Today, it hosts 9,000 inhabitants, and hundreds of recently built residences climb the green velvet slopes that cloak the throats of vast red rock formations. Elegant hotels, bed-and-breakfasts, galleries, and shops cater to uncountable tourists. Sedona's boom has also been augmented by the alleged discovery by New Age believers that several of the area's landforms, including a vast butte called Cathedral Rock, demonstrate great vortices of world-healing power.

Throughout the Southwest, ghost towns abound, particularly mining towns that went bust, but several of these found new lives after the veins of copper, gold, and silver ran out. The most startling, perhaps, is Jerome, perched improbably on the 30-degree slope of Mingus Mountain in Arizona. Once its mining days were numbered, it was saved by people bent on preserving its buildings of stone and wood, and was repopulated by artists and craftspeople. So precipitous is Jerome's terrain that residents grew accustomed to buildings sliding downhill. On one occasion, a movie theater slipped two feet but the projector kept running and the audience barely noticed. The chamber of commerce happily dubbed Jerome "A town on the move!"

Then there is Santa Fe, which never came close to being a ghost town. The city of Holy Faith, Santa Fe is the oldest capital city (1610) in what is now the United States and has been a magnet over the centuries to conquistadors and mountain men, a mecca for artists, craftspeople, pilgrims of all faiths, for writers, for Texans bent on culture, Californians bent on escape, and now even filmmakers.

Often considered a major travel destination, thanks in part to the architectural efforts that began early this century, Santa Fe has also been called, by one jaded critic from New York City, "an adobe theme park."

Indeed, so successful has Santa Fe been over the years that tourist facilities and the influx of ever wealthier newcomers have inflated property values beyond the reach of low-income people, including old Hispanic families, store clerks, waiters and waitresses, not to mention the city's fabled artists and craftspeople. It is classic boomtown economics, mixed with a zealous effort to protect "The Look" in the city's historic areas. All this can lead to exclusivity, even elitism.

In the early 1990s, Santa Fe was a deeply troubled city of some 60,000 people. The diverse cultures were not getting along. Hispanics and Anglos had lived side by side as recently as the 1970s and early 1980s—but no more.

In 1994, the city elected a Hispanic woman named Debbie Jaramillo as mayor. With a phrase-maker's talent, she galvanized many with her comment: "We painted our downtown brown and moved the brown people out." But her chief concern was not so much ethnic as economic, and the major thrust of her administration was to serve the whole community. This meant providing low-cost housing. Working with nonprofit charities, local builders and lenders, and prominent private foundations, she instigated the building of a large cluster of affordable houses and apartments in the still-uninflated southern edge of the city. Down-payment assistance and low-interest loans were made available to 5,000 potential homeowners, as well as loans for small business start-ups to stimulate local crafts and cottage industries—what she calls a "homegrown economy."

None of this attempt to preserve living history and community, as well as old buildings and "The Look," was accomplished without controversy, nor can anyone predict the future—even in Santa Fe. But to anyone who sees the Southwest as a place where widely differing ethnic groups can get along, even honor one another, while perhaps not fully understanding each other, the Jaramillo administration was a hopeful sign.

Outside the cities of the Southwest, there are counties the size of the smaller eastern states but with fewer than 5,000 inhabitants. Travelers visiting the Havasupai Indian reservation on the south rim of the Grand Canyon, for example, leave Seligman, Arizona (a proud remnant of the old days of Route 66, with its diners and geegaw shops), and head north across an ocean of undulating sage scrublands, an almost eerie drive of more than an hour without a sign of human habitation. A drive of similar length through Westchester County, New York, for example, would bring the driver within shouting distance of hundreds of thousands. But here, reaching a large parking lot seemingly perched on the edge of nowhere, the visitor goes on foot or on horseback down a thousand-foot cliff and another eight miles through dry washes and side canyons to the Indian town of Supai, famous for its glowing green waterfalls and said to be the only place in the United States where the mail is delivered by mule.

Or one can hike through the Mogollon Mountains in *(Continued on page 188)*

SON OF PAINTERS *Peter Hurd and Henriette Wyeth, artist Michael Hurd strolls*

with his dog near Las Cruces, New Mexico, under the great, inspiring bowl of sky.

IN A BOOTH *at the Palace of the Governors in Santa Fe (above),*
aficionados and connoisseurs attending the annual Indian Market examine rugs
woven by members of the Ramah Navajo Reservation weavers' cooperative.
Sponsored by the Southwestern Association for Indian Arts,
Indian Market is the largest exposition of authentic Indian wares
in the nation and has long played a major role in maintaining the vibrancy
and excellence of Indian arts and crafts. Santa Fe also hosts the annual
Spanish Market, where Hispanic artisans display and
sell their traditional crafts. These range from wooden carvings
of the saints and the Holy Family, called santos,
to furniture, paintings, and joyous tinwork, such as this cross
by Emilio and Senaida Romero (opposite).

THE TROMPE-L'OEIL perspective of a Taos mural by George Chacón, showing a woodcarver

at work on a gnarled piece of cedar, puts viewers in a state of uncertainty about reality.

*FACING white water,
uncertain weather, and all the other
hazards of river runners,
these intrepid adventurers embark
on a nine-day journey down the
Pecos River. Eight miles downriver
from their put-in point at
Pandale, Texas, the Pecos snakes
its way through a long stretch
of steep-sided canyons. Much of the
trip will be through remote and
unforgiving country. Along the way
they will fetch up near
the place where Judge Roy Bean,
"the law west of the Pecos,"
dispensed turn-of-the-century
justice from the porch of his saloon.
The hardships of the journey
will be tempered with a fair
supply of beer, and a freezer chest
of CDs will supply whatever
atmospherics are missing.*

*THOUGH HIS JOB driving an oil truck takes Keith McBee far from home,
all roads lead back to Odessa, Texas, and his daughter, KaSandra.*

(*Continued from page 179*) New Mexico, home of the first designated wilderness area
in the United States, thanks largely to the advocacy of Aldo Leopold. (Long before
he wrote his appeal for a "land ethic" in *Sand County Almanac,* the noted ecolo-
gist worked as a forest ranger in these mountains.) In the Mogollons, as well as in
numerous other mountain ranges, and along the great highlands of Arizona's mid-
section, a hiker can still go for days without coming across another human being.

Much of the Southwest's open land is in the public domain, to one degree or
another. In all, between military lands, those administered by the National Park
Service, the Forest Service, Bureau of Reclamation, Bureau of Land Management,
and other federal agencies, some 40 percent of the land area of New Mexico and
Arizona is owned by the federal government. Approximately another 20 percent
is within Indian reservations and thus, titularly, federal land. Here, as in Nevada,
Idaho, and the District of Columbia, the federal presence is ubiquitous.

It is no secret that in many parts of the United States, there is a love-hate rela-
tionship with the federal government, and nowhere more so than in the Western
rangelands. As elsewhere in what is called the New West, the postwar influx of
newcomers to the Southwest brought a new definition of the word "conservation."
Traditionally, in the West, it meant *use.* It was thought foolish to let a resource like
a river flow past you without using it, or to let grasslands go ungrazed. But the new
breed of conservationists mean something quite different—essentially preser-

vation of resources in their natural or wild state, as little trammeled as possible.

Generations of ranchers, for example, had leased huge tracts in the national forests and on other federal lands for grazing—and in many parts of the West, overgrazing was common. A fundamental conflict soon arose between environmentalists (including scientists) and ranchers. Both sides were furious with federal agencies who did either too little or too much. It was, and remains in most areas, a situation where a great deal of heat gives off very little light.

In the mid-1990s, a new approach began to glimmer in one of the least populated places in the entire Southwest, a country of scrubby and hostile desert flora and sparse grasslands where the borders of New Mexico, Arizona, and Mexico meet. There, in an area of about one million acres or so (almost the size of Delaware), some 100 people live on 35 ranches. Many of these ranches have been in the same families for four generations. Telephones reached the Arizona side of this area only in the 1980s, and until about 1990, the ranchers had to use their own generators for electricity. It is, today, a quiet place, where the vast open spaces are matched by an oceanic silence.

Among the holdings on the New Mexico side was Gray Ranch, in all some 320,000 acres (almost half the size of Rhode Island), with its own mountain range—the Animas—and a single pasture three times the size of Manhattan Island. In 1990, the Nature Conservancy bought Gray Ranch from an absentee Mexican cattle company for a reported 18 million dollars, bent on preserving the ranch's six different ecozones and nearly 20 endangered and threatened species. The locals were suspicious, despite the Conservancy's protests that it would continue to run cattle on the ranch. Then, a wondrous confluence of events and insights took place.

The Nature Conservancy soon realized that buying up such huge places and sequestering them as fenced-off refuges was not a viable way to save the vast open lands of the West. No one had the money for that. At the same time, the local ranchers were painfully aware of the bad reputation held by cattle ranchers in the outside world, the danger being that pressures for regulation would put them out of business altogether. They might be forced to sell out to developers and see the open country subdivided into ten-acre ranchettes and second homes—a new kind of ghost town that was appearing throughout the Western states.

Rather than act defensively to each new wave of grazing regulations, some of the locals formed the Malpai Borderlands Group. This was just about when the Nature Conservancy sold Gray Ranch to one of the more unusual locals—a man named Drum Hadley. An Anheuser Busch descendant and a poet, Hadley had been ranching in the area for 20 years. He and his family formed a foundation that purchased the Gray, making it a major part of the Malpai group, which began rethinking everything from the usual policy of putting out all lightning-ignited wildfires to the concept of environmentalists and ecologists as the enemy. They all, including the federal land agencies, shared a love of and devotion to open land; even land that is overgrazed can come back, but not if it is turned into exurbs. The Malpai ranchers had the idea of putting the adversaries together to talk about common goals. Knowing they needed sup-port, they invited the Nature Conservancy and scientists from the University of Arizona and elsewhere to participate.

By 1993, they had produced a "fire map" that showed the Forest Service and other agencies the places where ranchers wanted fires suppressed, where they wanted fires to burn freely, and areas they wanted to be consulted about when a fire broke out. The theory, of course, was that fire was one of the natural processes that created the grasslands over the eons and, without it, woody species like mesquite would spread at the expense of grass. In 1994, they set out to organize a burn, but it took eight months for the agencies involved to cut away the accre-tions of their own policies. For example, though every endangered species in the region has evolved with fire, the U.S. Fish and Wildlife Service sees its mission as protecting each such species and not letting it singe. But the burn finally took place, with the desired affect. Grasses grew in due course.

Meanwhile Drum Hadley had taken possession of Gray Ranch and was over-seeing his own burns. First he fenced off a large area until enough grass grew to provide fuel. Then, as sometimes happens, lightning struck and a fire burned, killing almost 30 percent of the unwanted plants. Microbes later overcame those the fire had wounded. In three years, the area was back in lush, stirrup-high grasses.

This grazing area is so large that one rancher can have a drought while others are unaffected. Hadley came up with a revolutionary idea: a grassbank. If a rancher in the Malpai group was having a bad year, he could graze his herd on Gray Ranch, let his land weather the drought and his grass grow, in the meantime putting an equivalent amount of his land's value into easement to forestall forever the possibility of it being subdivided. Five ranchers availed themselves

FOURTH-GENERATION rancher of the Arizona borderlands, Warner Glenn and his wife, Wendy, helped organize an association of ranchers, scientists, and people from the environmental movement to make a rare cooperative effort to use — and conserve — open lands in the Southwest.

of the grassbank in its first few years, evidently to everyone's satisfaction.

Some of the neighbors were suspicious of this unholy alliance, but watched it all with great care. The Malpai Borderlands Group meanwhile pressed on and gained a good deal of national publicity. Throughout the West, ranching communities, local environmental groups, and local arms of national groups such as the Sierra Club saw the Damocles sword of subdivision coming closer and closer and began forming their own unholy alliances.

The millennium thus ends with hope that one of the most intractable problems in the region—and throughout the West—can be resolved. Another set of antagonistic cultures might even learn to cooperate with each other to their mutual benefit. John Wesley Powell, who so long ago understood that intelligent cooperation between ranchers and the government was essential to the successful settling of lands west of the 100th meridian, would no doubt permit himself a smile.

*A*ND WHAT OF THE FIRST ONES, the American Indian tribes of the Southwest? In the early years of the upstart American republic, the chief justice of the United States Supreme Court, John Marshall, noted that Indian tribes were nations within the nation. Since that time, the notion of Indian sovereignty has risen and fallen, and is currently on the rise.

Sovereignty is a term fraught with almost incalculable legal ramifications, and today, among the many phenomena playing a role in its fate, one is the controversial matter of Indian gaming. Casinos have proliferated on Indian land in the Southwest. They are deplored by many, of course, and are looked upon with normal greed by state legislatures as additional sources of revenue. In some cases, casinos have led to an unprecedented influx of cash for the tribes, money they can use for economic development and projects for the general welfare, such as building better schools, medical facilities, and recreation centers. The tribes have also created scholarship funds for young people to go to college and beyond.

Another phenomenon is related. In the 1970s, the University of New Mexico law school established a program to attract Indians from across the country and train them as lawyers. Many returned home to fight their peoples' battles in courts and legislatures. One of the new Indian lawyers, Kevin Gover, a Pawnee with a law firm in Albuquerque, was recently appointed Assistant Secretary for Indian Affairs in the U.S. Department of Interior.

Today there is a second generation of superbly trained Indian lawyers working in the American judicial system, using the many tools within that grand machine to look after the lives of Indian people. They are asserting and reasserting old rights over land and water and reviving old treaty obligations, working for the same rights that any people need to become self-sustaining communities in charge of their own destiny.

Nowhere on the continent will this happen sooner than in the sunstruck lands of the American Southwest, where people of bewilderingly diverse ways have struggled for so long to find their common humanity.

LUPINES BLANKET
the forest floor beneath a stand of
aspens, called "quakies"
by locals in Colorado for the way their
leaves dance in the breeze.
Aspens opportunistically recolonize
patches of pine and spruce forest
cleared by fires, and in the fall
light up the mountains with
a flamboyant gold.

*In the mountains near the headwaters of the Pecos River in New Mexico,
riders still have vistas of wilderness untrammeled as far as
the eye can see. Such experiences draw millions to the Southwest each
year to visit. Some of these visitors, entranced by the style of life they find,
will get dressed in a proper outfit, find a hat that
suits (opposite), and stay for good.*

LITTLE OBSCURED by the lights of Phoenix a hundred miles away, the stars

wheel overhead in a time exposure made along Arizona's fabled Devil's Highway.

INDEX

Boldface indicates illustrations.

NOTES ON THE CONTRIBUTORS

BRUCE DALE was a NATIONAL GEOGRAPHIC staff photographer for more than 30 years, during which time he was twice named Magazine Photographer of the Year by the National Press Photographers Association. Among the many subjects he covered for NATIONAL GEOGRAPHIC magazine were John Wesley Powell, the Pecos River, Geronimo's Southwest, and the Santa Fe Trail. Two books for the Society, *Gypsies* and *American Mountain People*, offered an intimate look into these cultures. Since leaving the staff in 1994, Dale has worked mainly on advertising and special assignment photography. He has taught a number of photo workshops, and for the past three summers has led one along the Pecos River in New Mexico.

JAKE PAGE has written about the Southwest for a number of publications, including NATIONAL GEOGRAPHIC and NATIONAL GEOGRAPHIC TRAVELER. He has published articles on history, culture, nature, politics, and science in *Smithsonian, Preservation, Air & Space*, and other publications, and has written five mystery novels and two historical novels, all of them set in the Southwest. With his wife, photographer Susanne Page, he produced *Hopi* (1982) and *Navajo* (1996). Their most recent collaboration is *A Field Guide to Southwestern Indian Arts and Crafts* (1998). Page lives in New Mexico with his wife.

ACKNOWLEDGMENTS

The Book Division wishes to thank the individuals, groups, and organizations named or quoted in the text. In addition, we are grateful for the assistance of Russ Bodnar, Elizabeth M. Brouwers, LoRheda Fry, Wendy Glenn, Doug Hardy, May Lee, John Mangimeli, Bruce McCabe, David Moore, Will Morris, Ellen Seeley, Ren A. Thompson, and Warren Wagner.

ADDITIONAL READING

The reader may wish to consult the *National Geographic Index* for related articles and books, in particular National Geographic's *Guide to the National Parks of the United States.* The following titles are also recommended: Edward Abbey, *Desert Solitaire: A Season in the Wilderness;* Kenneth A. Brown, *Four Corners: History, Land, and People of the Desert Southwest;* Lawrence Cheek, *Arizona;* Michael S. Durham, *The Desert States: Smithsonian Guide to Historic America;* Frederick R. Gehlbach, *Mountain Islands and Desert Seas: A Natural History of the U.S.-Mexican Borderlands;* Nancy Harbert, *New Mexico;* James A. MacMahon, *Deserts;* Susanne and Jake Page, *Field Guide to Southwest Indian Arts and Crafts;* Stephen Plog, *Ancient Peoples of the American Southwest;* William E. Riebsame, editor, *Atlas of the New West;* Zdenek Salzmann and Joy Salzmann, *Native Americans of the Southwest;* Marc Simmons, *New Mexico: An Interpretive History;* Edward H. Spicer, *The Cycles of Conquest: The Impact of Spain, Mexico, and the United States on the Indians of the Southwest, 1533-1960;* John Upton Terrell, *The Man Who Rediscovered America;* Philip Varney, *Arizona Ghost Towns and Mining Camps;* George Wuerthner, *Grand Canyon: A Visitor's Companion.*

Library of Congress Cataloging-in-Publication Data

Page, Jake.
    The American Southwest : land of challenge and promise / by Jake Page ; photographed by Bruce Dale.
        p.   cm.
    Includes index.
    ISBN 0-7922-7063-0. —ISBN 0-7922-7067-3 (dlx.)
    1. Southwest, New—Description and travel. 2. Southwest, New-History. I. Dale, Bruce. II. Title.
F787.P34 1998
979—dc21
98-5493   CIP

Composition for this book by the National Geographic Society Book Division. Set in Goudy. Map production by GeoSystems, Lancaster, Pa. Color separations by Digital Color Image, Pennsauken, N.J. Printed and bound by R. R. Donnelley & Sons, Willard, Ohio. Dust jacket printed by Miken Systems, Inc., Cheektowaga, N.Y.